SO-AUE-573

7.14.80

THE ATHLETE'S COOKBOOK

Easy Recipes and Nutritional Guidelines for Active People

By Marilyn Shope Peterson and Charlene S. Martinsen
Illustrated by Wayland Moore

THE ATHLETE'S COOKBOOK

Easy Recipes and Nutritional Guidelines for Active People

By Marilyn Shope Peterson and Charlene S. Martinsen
Illustrated by Wayland Moore

Smuggler's Cove Publishing
Seattle

Printed in the United States of America.

Library of Congress Cataloging in Publication Data

Peterson, Marilyn Shope, 1935—
    The Athlete's Cookbook.

    Bibliography: p.
    Includes index.
    1. Athletes—Nutrition. 2. Cookery.
I. Martinsen, Charlene S., joint author.
II. Moore, Wayland. III. Title.
TX361.A8P47   641.5'63   79-9658

ISBN 0-918484-05-7

Published by Smuggler's Cove Publishing
          107 West John St.
          Seattle, Washington 98119
          (206) 285-3171

Cover design: Ben Dennis
Cover illustration: Wayland Moore
Book design: Jane Bailey
Editing: Betsy Case, Jane Bailey
Typestyle: Kabel, set by Debbie Higgins and Kim Field

To the athletes in our lives!

Contents

Every so often someone comes along with an idea so different and interesting that one is inclined to ask, "Why didn't I think of that first?" A cookbook for athletes is just such an idea. Having spent more than thirty years coaching I can attest to the fact that eating the proper things at the right time is of fundamental importance to successful performance.

Marilyn Peterson and Charlene Martinsen are professionals having wide experience in nutritional counseling, meal planning and food preparation. A mother of four active children, Marilyn has worked with athletes ranging from novice to world class ability. She has been a consultant to both men's and women's teams, including high school, university and Olympic team candidates at the national training centers: Squaw Valley, California and Colorado Springs, Colorado. Charlene Martinsen teaches in Nutritional Sciences at the University of Washington. She has written many cookbooks, including the bestseller, **Gourmet Grains**.

The Athlete's Cookbook is a practical nutritional guide for parents, coaches and athletes. Perhaps its greatest value is its simplicity and usefulness in meal planning on a daily basis.

Kenneth E. Foreman, Ph.D.
Head Coach United States Olympic Team
Women's Athletics, 1980

Cooking for athletes is a challenge! From young swimmers, to early-morning joggers, to football champions...they are delighted with imaginative, energy-packed meals. However, busy schedules often prevent athletes from spending enough time to prepare and eat the right foods. For bodies operating at top performance levels, the proper balance of fluids, calories and carbohydrates is essential. The recipes in this book contribute to maximum performance, tempt the fussiest player...and are appropriate for the entire family.

Each recipe has been tested by the authors, their families, friends and athletic acquaintances. Some of the dishes are low calorie, some high in calories. Many take 15 minutes or less to prepare. And, all are delicious! They fit an athlete's lifestyle, tastebuds and nutritional needs...and provide that extra energy boost necessary for winning, or just keeping in shape.

The game jargon is one of the tools you need to play football, tennis or any other sport. These words often don't mean much in themselves but in the context of the athletic event they take on special meanings. Jargon words are short cuts to communication and an outsider feels left out without these tools. Like the sports, nutrition has its own jargon. Most of the words are familiar but they have a special meaning when applied to athletic performance.

Alcohol: An ingredient in a variety of beverages, including beer, wine, liqueurs, cordials and mixed or straight drinks. Pure alcohol itself yields about 7 calories per gram, of which more than 75% is available to the body. The mature athlete may enjoy a beer after the run or workout. But, because of its efficient absorption rate and the adverse side effects, the developing athlete should not consume alcohol.

Calorie: A unit used to express the heat or energy value of food. Calories in food come from carbohydrate, protein, fat, and alcohol.

Carbohydrate: One of three major sources of energy in foods. The most common carbohydrates are sugars and starches. For each gram of carbohydrate you eat, your body gets about 4 calories. Scientists have been able to show that the consumption of high carbohydrate meals is beneficial to the athlete participating in endurance events.

Carbohydrate Loading: A method of increasing carbohydrate consumption, also called glycogen loading. We store carbohydrate in our muscles and liver as glycogen. When more glycogen is stored in the muscle, more energy is available for the athlete to use. It has been shown that if an athlete decreases muscle glycogen by exercising strenuously and eating a diet low in carbohydrate, then relaxes and eats a diet high in carbohydrate for several days, glycogen, the storage form of carbohydrate, will be increased in the muscle. For example, a swimmer might work out intensely for several days, eating foods high in protein and fat and keeping the carbohydrates in his diet low. Then for the next few days, the swimmer eats foods high in carbohydrate and cuts down on exercise by concentrating on turns or entry into the water. With an increase in muscle glycogen, the swimmer will be able to swim longer. It is important to remember that an athlete will not win just by concentrating on carbohydrate foods. Winning is more than just a diet routine. However, it has been documented that an increased glycogen store in the muscles is an advantage in endurance activities.

Cholesterol: A fat-like substance present in blood, muscle, liver, brain and all other tissues throughout the body of man and animals and, therefore, in foods of animal origin. Cholesterol is a key part of the fatty deposits in the arterial wall in atherosclorosis.

Energy: The heat provided from food which is necessary for work. Each food contains protein, carbohydrate, fat or a combination of these nutrients which are available for energy production. The energy needs of the body are the first priority of life. Before anything else can happen, like growth or repair, basic energy needs must be met. If an athlete's diet is composed mainly of protein, then his body will use protein for energy. If the diet does not supply enough total calories, protein and fat from body tissues will be used to provide the needed energy to go through the long day of training. When the athlete uses his body as a source of food, he loses weight. This may be desirable in sports such as wrestling and gymnastics. Fasting should be discouraged, however, as the body's stores provide only calories and not vitamins, minerals, or sufficient fluids.

Enrichment: The addition of one or more nutrients to a food in order to increase the consumption of those nutrients. The nutrients added to the food are often nutrients already present in the food that have been lost by processing. The best example of enrichment is the addition of B vitamins to white bread or flour. When nutrients are added to a food at a level that is higher than normally found in the food, the food is said to be fortified.

Fat: One of three major energy sources in food. Fat yields about 9 calories per gram. A major emphasis in athletics, with the exception of distance swimming, is to reduce total body fat. This is done by training and reducing the amount of fat in the diet. A general recommendation is to keep the percent of calories from fat less than 30% of total calories in the diet.

Fiber: An indigestible part of fruits, vegetables, cereals and grains. Fiber is important in the diet as roughage or bulk.

Food Exchange: Foods grouped together on a list according to similarities in food values. Measured amounts of foods within the group may be used as "trade-offs" for each other in planning meals. An exchange contains similar amounts of calories, carbohydrates, proteins, fats, minerals and vitamins.

Food Habit: The usual pattern of an individual or group in choosing, preparing and eating. Food habits result from family, cultural, economic and religious influences.

Fortification: The addition of one or more nutrients to a food whether or not they are naturally present, and/or at levels higher than those naturally present. The terms "vitamin added" or "with added vitamins and minerals" as well as the term "fortified" have been used to identify fortified products.

Glycogen: A storage form of carbohydrate found in animal tissue. The body makes glycogen from glucose and stores it in limited amounts in the liver and muscles. Normal storage provides approximately 1½ hours of energy to work at 65% maximum effort.

Gram: A unit of mass in the metric system. An ounce is 28.25 grams.

Mineral: A substance required in small amounts to build and repair body tissue and/or control functions of the body. Calcium, iron, magnesium, phosphorus, potassium, sodium, and zinc are minerals. The iron stores of female distance runners are usually low and therefore should be supplemented.

Monounsaturated Fat: A fat that contains a low degree of unsaturation.

Nutrient: A substance in food necessary for life: protein, fats, carbohydrates, minerals, vitamins and water. There are approximately 50 known nutrients the human body needs in order to survive that must be supplied by the foods eaten. Nutrients provide energy to keep us warm, to help our organs function, to help us think, move and work, to help our bodies use the food we eat, to help the growth process, and to help replace worn-out or damaged cells. These nutritional building blocks are designed to work in team formation. As with the members of a team, one combination of nutrients is often better in a specific situation. For example, eggs are a good source of the iron we need in our blood. If orange juice, which contains Vitamin C, is included in the same meal, the Vitamin C enhances the iron absorption. Another example of how nutrients work together is found in milk. Milk is fortified with Vitamin D because it helps our body use calcium. All foods contain a variety of nutrients, but there is no food which contains all the nutrients we need. The best approach is to eat a variety of foods at one time. Then the chance of getting optimum nutrition without supplementation is very good.

Nutrition: A combination of processes by which the body receives and uses the materials necessary for energy, growth, tissue replacement, and maintenance of body functions.

Polyunsaturated Fats: Fats from vegetables such as corn, cottonseed, sunflower, safflower and soybean oil. Oils high in polyunsaturated fats have more double bonds and may be beneficial in lowering blood cholesterol levels.

Protein: A major nutrient in foods made up of amino acids that are essential for the life processes. Protein provides about 4 calories per gram. Protein has always received lots of attention from athletes. Often developing athletes eat lots of protein from foods or from supplements because they want larger muscles. Certainly some extra protein over the amount needed for normal functions is needed to lay down muscle tissue. A safe recommendation is 1 to 1½ grams of protein for every kilogram of body weight. The athlete, with his increased need for extra calories, usually will supply enough extra protein by just eating more food. If consuming extra protein is part of your dietary regimen, remember that extra water is required to dispose of the metabolic by-products uric acid and urea. If this is not done, diarrhea and loss of appetite as well as weight loss may occur. Animal foods such as the egg or milk are the most utilizable form of protein.

Saturated Fat: Fat that is often hard at room temperature. It is primarily from animal food products (like butter, lard, meat fat). Saturated fat may raise the level of cholesterol in the blood.

Sodium: An element essential for neural transport and basic body functions. Although athletes lose large amounts of sodium with sweat, the average lightly salted meal will replace this loss. Any excess of sodium, often experienced with salt tablets, will cause dehydration and cramping.

Supplement: Addition of any nutrient in the amount not found in the food intake. Vitamin/mineral supplements are justified during intestinal malabsorption (diarrhea), low calorie intake or when food does not supply the amount of nutrient needed by the individual. Calcium and iron are often recommended as supplements to the diet of female endurance athletes. Bee pollen, wheat germ, brewer's yeast, and various other combinations are also sold as supplements to the diet. While these products do contain small amounts of various nutrients, they don't contain much else. Scientists have not found that any of these products improve performance.

Vitamin: Substance essential in small amounts to assist in body processes and functions. The major vitamins include A, D, E, the B complex and C.

Water: The most essential nutrient. Water is of particular concern to the athlete as dehydration is a special problem for athletes. It is necessary for energy production, temperature control and the elimination of by-products of cell metabolism.

The Pre-Event Meal

A special meal is traditionally eaten during the hours before the event when an athlete is preparing mentally and physically for competition. This is the time to build up team comradery and concentration on winning.

Many legends about winning include the meals particular athletes have eaten before victory. Two-pound pregame steaks gave the football coach of yesterday confidence that his team could handle the demands of the game and emerge victorious! We now know that for the energy an athlete needs during competition the carbohydrate content of the pre-event meal is more important than the amount of protein it contains.

These are the general guidelines athletes should remember when chowing down before a game.

1. The timing of the meal is important! A mixed diet generally takes two to three hours to leave the stomach. Food in the stomach requires an increased flow of blood to that area, while increased exercise demands an increased flow of blood to the working muscles. With only five liters of blood, there just isn't enough to carry out both functions well. So don't eat and run! During warm weather the problem is compounded because the capillaries grow larger to help cool the body, increasing the require-

ments for blood even more. So plan to eat at least three hours before the event.

2. The meal should include favorite foods...this psychological benefit is always helpful.

3. The meal should be attractively served in a relaxed atmosphere...another important psychological benefit.

4. Foods should be easily digestible to minimize gastric upset. Avoid the cabbage and bean families, hot peppers and those baskets of greasy fish and chips! Concentrate on simple casseroles and broiled foods.

5. Include two or three glasses of non-fat, non-carbonated fluids. This includes any kind of juice, low-fat milk or water.

6. If the pre-event meal is an away-from-home affair, remember that the typical restaurant meal is high in fat and protein...and low in necessary carbohydrates. Pre-plan the meal from the standard menu, or ask the restaurant to prepare a special meal. Many restaurants are happy to cooperate. All they need is a little extra time.

7. And, even if the meal is being paid for by someone else...don't overeat. A full stomach slows any athlete down!

Some of the best competitive swimmers are teenagers who need calories to grow and train. They rarely have time between workouts, school and activities to run home to mom's cooking. The answer to their hit-and-miss diet is a breakfast with imagination.

After any breakfast, the swimmer will have a better early morning workout, and will continue to perform well during the day. Often swimmers, especially women, who spend hours in form-fitting tank suits, think they should cut back on calories to lose weight during the competitive season. This is not the time to skip meals...strength, energy and concentration at the starting block come from a well-balanced diet.

To tempt a swimmer into the breakfast habit...whip up one of the following lively, light meals or a frothy breakfast milkshake.

Light Breakfast Menus for Swimmers

Breakfast in a Glass**
Toast

Orange Juice
Applesauce Toast**

Apple Juice
Corn-off-the-Cob Hot Cereal**

Recipes from Swimmers:

Alice Browne's Carrot Cake*
  World Class Swimmer with the Mission Viejo
  Nadadores

Brian Goodell's Red Noodles*
  World record holder in the 1500 meter and the
  800 meter freestyle

**In this chapter
*See Index

Pineapple Smash

2 c water (480 ml)
1 c sugar (240 ml)
2 c grated or crushed pineapple (480 ml)
½ c lemon juice (120 ml)
6 ice cubes
1 pt pineapple sherbet (480 ml)
1 qt ginger ale (1 liter)
Mint

Mix first five ingredients in blender until ice is slushed. Divide into eight glasses. Add a scoop of sherbet and enough gingerale to fill glass. Serve with a sprig of mint.

Serves 8.

Calories per serving: approximately 290.

Breakfast in a Glass

1 egg
⅓ c frozen orange juice concentrate (80 ml)
¼ c powdered milk (60 ml)
½ banana
¾ c water or milk (180 ml)
4 ice cubes

Place all ingredients in a blender and blend for 1 minute. Pour into a chilled glass. Serve.

Serves 2.

Calories per serving: approximately 200.

Mountain Sunshine

½ c honey (120 ml)
½ c orange juice (120 ml)
3 Tbsp lemon juice (45 ml)
10 oz evaporated milk (280 g)
12 oz apricot nectar (340 g)

Blend all ingredients well. Chill and pour in cold thermos.

Serves 2.

Calories per serving: approximately 550.

Yogurt Milk Shake

8 oz carton of plain yogurt
1 c orange juice
1 ripe banana, cut into pieces
2 Tbsp honey

Place all ingredients in blender and blend until smooth. Pour into chilled glass.

Serves 2.

Calories per serving: approximately 300.

Phoenix Sunshine

½ c carrot juice (120 ml)
¼ c pineapple juice (60 ml)
½ c milk (120 ml)
2 tsp honey (10 ml)

Mix in the blender and serve over ice. Makes 1 serving, but if you use the individual sized cans of juice, there will be enough for your little brother.

Calories per serving: approximately 200.

Orange Cooler

¼ c frozen orange juice concentrate (60 ml)
¾ c ice water (180 ml)
1 pt lemon sherbet (480 ml)
12 oz gingerale (360 ml)

Place orange juice, ice water and sherbet in a blender and blend for 15 seconds. Divide among 4 chilled glasses. Add ¼ of the gingerale to each glass. Stir and serve immediately.

Serves 4.

Calories per serving: approximtely 210.

Blueberry Shake

1 c blueberry pie filling (240 ml)
1 pt vanilla ice cream (480 ml)
1 c milk (240 ml)
1 tsp lemon juice (5 ml)

Place all ingredients in blender. Blend for 10 seconds. Pour into chilled glasses.

Serves 3.

Calories per serving: approximately 400.

Peach Shake

1 c sliced fresh peaches (240 ml)
¼ c frozen lemonade concentrate (60 ml)
2 Tbsp sugar (30 ml)
1 pt vanilla ice cream (480 ml)
1 c milk (240 ml)

Combine all ingredients in a blender until smooth (10-15 seconds). Pour into chilled glass and serve.

Serves about 3.

Calories per serving: approximately 350.

Pink Strawberry Fruit Float

1 c strawberries, washed and hulled (240 ml)
2 Tbsp sugar (30 ml)
1 c vanilla ice cream (240 ml)
1 c milk (240 ml)

Puree strawberries and sugar in blender. Pour into 2 glasses, add milk to each glass, stir and top with a scoop of ice cream. Variation: use fresh peaches, 2 Tbsp lemon juice and sugar. Add orange juice to fill and top with peach ice cream.

Serves 2.

Calories per serving: approximately 370.

Corn-Off-The-Cob Hot Cereal

¼ c yellow cornmeal (60 ml)
¼ c cold water (60 ml)
2 tsp wheat germ (10 ml)
¾ c boiling water (180 ml)
¼ c powdered milk (60 ml)
¼ c cottage cheese (60 ml)
2 Tbsp honey (30 ml)
1 Tbsp butter (15 ml)

Mix together cornmeal, cold water and wheat germ. Bring ¾ c water to boil, add cornmeal and powdered milk. Stir constantly about 2 minutes. Pour into bowl. Top with cottage cheese, honey and butter.

Serves 1 - 2.

Calories per serving: approximately 330.

Sodium and Potassium Replacement

6 oz orange juice concentrate (180 g)
6 oz limeade or lemonade concentrate (180 g)
3 Tbsp lemon or lime juice (45 ml)
2 Tbsp honey or sugar (30 ml)
Pinch of salt
2 qt cold water (2 liters)

Mix all ingredients. Sip slowly in 3 oz (90 ml) portions. This drink has approximately the same amount of potassium and sodium as commercial preparations.

Calories per serving: approximately 25.

All-Star French Toast

1 c all-purpose flour (240 ml)
1½ tsp baking powder (7 ml)
½ tsp salt (3 ml)
1 c milk (240 ml)
2 eggs
8 slices whole wheat bread

Strawberry Cream Dip

1 c whipping cream, whipped (120 ml)
3 Tbsp sugar (45 ml)
½ tsp vanilla (3 ml)
½ c sliced strawberries (120 ml)

Mix flour, baking powder, salt, milk and eggs. Dip bread and fry on greased grill until light brown on both sides. Keep warm on rack in oven until ready to serve. Whip cream with sugar and vanilla. Serve on toast topped with strawberries. Maple syrup, flavored with Grand Marnier can be used instead of the cream topping.

Serves 4.

Calories per serving: approximately 575.

Breakfast Ideas

Prepare your favorite oatmeal following the package directions. Peel and mash bananas, allowing about half a banana and 1 Tbsp raisins per serving. Add bananas and raisins to cooked oatmeal. Serve with brown sugar and milk.

Calories per serving: approximately 275.

Applesauce Toast

1 Tbsp margarine (15 ml)
1½ Tbsp brown sugar (22 ml)
1 c applesauce (240 ml)
Cinnamon and nutmeg to taste
4 slices whole wheat toast

Melt margarine and combine with sugar, applesauce, cinnamon and nutmeg. Spread evenly on toast. Warm under broiler until bubbly, or cook in microwave for 30 seconds.

Serves 4.

Calories per serving: approximately 140.

Whole Wheat and Soy Waffles

1 c whole wheat flour (240 ml)
¼ c soy flour (60 ml)
1 tsp salt (5 ml)
2 tsp baking powder (10 ml)
2 eggs, separated
1½ c milk (360 ml)
3 Tbsp oil (45 ml)
2 Tbsp honey (30 ml)
1 tsp vanilla (5 ml)

Preheat waffle iron. Stir together the 2 kinds of flour and the salt and baking powder. Beat egg yolks until they are light yellow; add milk, oil, honey and vanilla. Blend well and stir into the dry ingredients. Beat egg whites until stiff, and fold into batter. Pour about ¾ c (180 ml) or enough for 1 waffle onto the hot waffle iron. Bake until golden brown. Serve with maple syrup or warmed brown sugar and honey.

Makes about 4 waffles.

Calories per serving: approximately 130.

Wheat Germ Pancakes

½ c wheat germ (120 ml)
1 c flour (240 ml)
2½ tsp baking powder (12 ml)
½ tsp salt (3 ml)
1 Tbsp sugar (15 ml)
1¼ c buttermilk (300 ml)
1 Tbsp honey (15 ml)
½ c small-curd cottage cheese (120 ml)

Toast wheat germ in oven at 350°F (175°C) for 5 minutes or until slightly brown. Sift flour with baking powder, salt and sugar. Add wheat germ. Combine milk, oil and honey and stir into dry ingredients. Stir in cottage cheese. Batter will be slightly lumpy. Drop by spoonfuls onto griddle; turn when bubbles appear.

Makes 12 pancakes, but may be doubled or tripled easily.

Calories per serving: approximately 120.

Cheese Bran Waffles

2 c sifted all-purpose flour (480 ml)
1 Tbsp baking powder (15 ml)
1 tsp salt (5 ml)
¾ c bran flake cereal (180 ml)
¾ c shredded sharp Cheddar cheese (180 ml)
2 eggs, separated
1½ c milk (360 ml)
¼ c melted shortening (60 ml)

Sift flour, baking powder and salt. Stir in bran flake cereal and cheese. Add egg yolks, milk and shortening to flour mixture. Stir until well blended. Beat egg whites until stiff and fold into batter. Pour about ¾ c (180 ml) onto hot waffle iron. Bake until golden brown. Serve with syrup or fresh fruit.

Makes 4 to 6 large waffles.

Calories per serving: approximately 400.

Oatmeal Fruit Coffee Cake

1 c chopped dried apricots (240 ml)
2 c sifted all-purpose flour (480 ml)
½ c sugar (120 ml)
2½ tsp baking powder (13 ml)
½ tsp baking soda (3 ml)
1 tsp salt (5 ml)
1 c quick-cooking rolled oats (240 ml)
1¼ c buttermilk (300 ml)
1 egg
¼ c oil (60 ml)
½ c chopped nuts (120 ml)

Place apricots in a saucepan, cover with water and bring to a simmer. Drain and set fruit aside. Sift flour, sugar, baking powder, baking soda and salt together. Mix in oatmeal. In a bowl, blend buttermilk, egg, and oil. Add milk mixture, apricots and nuts to flour mixture and stir until just blended. Pour into greased 8 × 8-inch (19 X 19 cm) pan and bake at 350°F (175°C) for 40 minutes or until done.

Serves 9.

Calories per serving: approximately 320.

Breakfast Shortcake. Why Not?

1 qt strawberries (1 liter)
½ c sugar (120 ml)
2 c flour (480 ml)
2 Tbsp sugar (30 ml)
1 Tbsp baking powder (15 ml)
1 tsp salt (5 ml)
⅓ c shortening (80 ml)
1 c milk (240 ml)
½ tsp lemon peel (3 ml)
2 c whipping cream, whipped (480 ml)

Slice strawberries; sprinkle with ½ c (120 ml) sugar. Measure flour, 2 Tbsp sugar (30 ml), baking powder, and salt into bowl. Cut in shortening thoroughly until mixture looks like meal. Stir in milk and lemon peel until blended. Pat into 8" circle on greased cookie sheet. Bake 15 minutes at 450 °F (225 °C). Split shortcake while warm; fill and top with berries. Serve warm with cream.

Serves 8.

Calories per serving: approximately 580.

Breakfast Pizza

2 English muffins
½ c tomato sauce (120 ml)
¼ c chopped ham or luncheon meat (60 g)
1 c Mozzarella cheese, grated (240 ml)

Lightly toast English muffins. Spread tomato sauce over each half of muffin. Sprinkle with meat and cheese. Broil about 5 minutes or until cheese is bubbly.

Serves 4.

Calories per serving: approximately 225.

Banana Sandwiches

4 slices white or whole wheat bread
2 to 4 Tbsp peanut butter (30 - 60 ml)
1 small banana

Toast bread. Spread with peanut butter. Slice banana and place on top of peanut butter. Top with slice of bread and slice each sandwich in half.

Makes 2 sandwiches.

Calories per serving: approximately 250.

Fruit Wheels

2 bagels
3 oz cream cheese (90 ml)
½ tsp ground cinnamon (3 ml)
2 fresh peaches
2 bananas

Split and toast 2 bagels (or toasted whole wheat bread may be used). Spread each with cream cheese; sprinkle with ground cinnamon. Thinly slice peaches and bananas and place on top of each bagel half.

Serves 4.

Calories per serving: approximately 200.

Franco Columbu's Mediterranean Omelet

4 eggs
1 pinch salt
1 pinch oregano
1 pinch pepper
4 large, ripe Italian olives
2 oz Provolone (60 g)
3 Tbsp butter (45 ml)

Beat eggs until foamy. Add salt, oregano and pepper. Pit olives and cut into pieces. Cut cheese into ½-inch pieces. Heat butter in 10-inch skillet. Add eggs and stir until nearly half cooked. Add olives and cheese and continue cooking until eggs are as firm as desired.

Serves 2.

Calories per serving: approximately 400.

Franco Columbu is an internationally known body builder.

Peanut Butter and Orange Sandwiches

1 orange, peeled, cut into bite-size pieces, or
    ½ c mandarin oranges (120 ml)
1 Tbsp orange juice (15 ml)
1 Tbsp honey (15 ml)
½ c peanut butter (120 ml)
6 slices whole wheat bread

Combine orange pieces, orange juice, honey and peanut butter, blending lightly. Spread on 3 slices of bread. Top with remaining bread and cut in half.

Makes 3 sandwiches.

Calories per serving: approximately 260.

Ham and Cheese Scramble

2 Tbsp butter (30 ml)
1 Tbsp oil (15 ml)
1 medium onion, chopped
½ c chopped cooked ham (70 g)
10 ½-oz condensed Cheddar cheese soup
   (315 g)
8 eggs, beaten

Heat butter and oil, add onion and saute until soft. Stir in ham. In a separate bowl, stir the soup until smooth, blend in beaten eggs. Place sauteed meat and onion in casserole and add egg mixture. Cover and bake in oven at 350⁰F (175⁰C) for 15 minutes, or until firm. May be baked in a microwave, following manufacturer directions.

Serves 6.

Calories per serving: approximately 270.

Swiss Breakfast Pie

1 c fine cracker crumbs (240 ml)
¼ c butter, melted (60 ml)
6 slices bacon, cooked crisp & crumbled
½ c chopped onion (120 ml)
3 eggs, slightly beaten
¾ c dairy sour cream (180 ml)
½ tsp dry mustard (3 ml)
½ tsp salt (3 ml)
Dash pepper
2 c Swiss cheese, shredded (480 ml)
¼ c finely chopped parsley (60 ml)

Combine cracker crumbs and butter; press into bottom and sides of 8-inch (19 cm) pie plate. Combine bacon, onion, eggs, sour cream, dry mustard, salt, pepper and Swiss cheese. Pour into pie shell. Bake at 375⁰F (185⁰C) for 25 to 30 minutes, or until knife comes out clean. Garnish with parsley. Let stand 5 minutes before cutting.

Serves 5 - 6.

Calories per serving: approximately 325.

Hockey players use up an estimated 15 calories a minute...and the game is 60 minutes long! Carrying 20 to 40 pounds of equipment, combined with the effort of keeping warm, helps hockey players keep trim without effort during the season...and they need even more calories during training. They can enjoy large, high calorie meals...meals that start with delightful appetizers! Pre-game meals should be eaten at least four hours before the game and include lots of carbohydrates for energy.

For younger competitors, a high calorie snack during breaks in training is beneficial. And whether the player is a pro, semi-pro or novice, a hot snack for the ride home is a welcome treat.

The recipes in this chapter can double as mouth-watering appetizers or after-game treats.

Celebration Cocktail Party

American System Cheese Dip**
Teriyaki Chestnuts**
Liver Pate**
Seattle Oyster Roll**
Pickled Salmon**
Jezebel Sauce and Cheese**
Mellow Yellow Cheese Sticks**
Crackers and Cheeses

Beverages

Fresh Lemonade
Milk or Tea
Coffee

**In this chapter

American System Cheese Dip

2 hard-cooked eggs
½ c canned green chilies (120 ml)
¼ c chopped ripe olives (60 ml)
1 lb sharp American cheese, grated (450 g)
¼ lb butter (120 g)
10 oz condensed tomato soup (300 g)
2 drops Tabasco sauce
½ tsp Worcestershire sauce (3 ml)
¼ tsp salt (1 ml)
¼ tsp pepper (1 ml)

Chop eggs and chilies and place in saucepan. Add olives, cheese, butter, tomato soup, Tabasco, Worcestershire, salt and pepper. Heat slowly until cheese is melted. Serve with bread cubes, toast strips or raw carrot sticks.

Makes 3 cups.

Calories per cup: approximately 1000.

Anchovy Prega

½ c butter (120 ml)
¼ c oil (60 ml)
4 small garlic cloves, mashed
¼ c chopped anchovy fillets (60 ml)
½ loaf French bread

Heat butter, oil and garlic until simmering. Add anchovies and simmer for 5 minutes. Serve warm with pieces of bread to dip in sauce.

Serves 4 as an appetizer.

Calories per serving: approximately 500.

Peanut Butter Appetizer

½ c peanut butter (120 ml)
2 Tbsp horseradish (30 ml)
12 - 2" (5 cm) squares of toast
¼ c chopped peanuts (60 ml)

Mix peanut butter and horseradish. Spread on toast. Garnish with chopped peanuts.

Serves 12, as hors d'oeuvres.

Calories per serving: approximately 100.

Blackeyed Pea Dip

8 oz Old English Sharp cheese, grated (240 g)
½ lb butter (240 g)
4 c cooked blackeyed peas (1 liter)
3 jalapeno peppers
1 Tbsp jalapeno pepper juice (15 ml)
½ medium onion, chopped
1 Tbsp chopped green chiles (15 ml)
1 clove garlic, minced

Melt cheese and butter over low heat. Mash peas and add with remaining ingredients. Stir pea mixture into melted cheese. Heat slowly. Serve with corn chips or raw vegetables such as carrot and celery sticks.

Makes 5 cups.

Calories per cup: approximately 1000.

Mexicali Dip

2 c cooked kidney beans, mashed (480 ml)
3 cloves garlic
½ tsp liquid hot-pepper seasoning (3 ml)
1 tsp Worcestershire sauce (5 ml)
¼ c mayonnaise (60 ml)
2 Tbsp lemon juice (30 ml)
1 Tbsp minced green onions (15 ml)

Place all ingredients in a blender and blend until smooth, about 60 seconds. Place in serving bowl and sprinkle with additional green onion slices if desired. Serve with carrot and celery sticks or tortilla chips.

Makes 2 cups.

Calories per Tbsp: approximately 40.

Jezebel Sauce and Cheese

1 c apple jelly (240 ml)
1 c pineapple preserves (240 ml)
¼ c creamed horseradish (60 ml)
2 tsp dry mustard (more if desired) (10 ml)
½ tsp black pepper (3 ml)
8 oz cream cheese (240 g)

Heat apple jelly and pineapple preserves until just melted. Add horseradish, dry mustard and black pepper. Spoon over cream cheese. Serve as a spread for dark rye bread or whole wheat crackers.

Serves 4-6.

Calories per Tbsp: approximately 75.

Teriyaki Chestnuts

5 oz water chestnuts (150 g)
¼ c soy sauce (60 ml)
¼ c honey (60 ml)
1 Tbsp sherry (optional) (15 ml)
4 large slices bacon

Drain water chestnuts and cut larger ones into pieces so you have altogether about 16 pieces of water chestnuts. Mix soy sauce, honey and sherry in a bowl and add water chestnuts. Marinate 30 minutes. Cut bacon slices in half lengthwise and crosswise and wrap each ¼ around a piece of chestnut, fastening with a toothpick. Bake at 400°F (200°C) for about 20 minutes or until bacon is crisp. Marinade can be saved and used as a basting sauce for chickens.

16 appetizers.

Calories per serving: approximately 35.

2112248

Seattle Oyster Roll

2 Tbsp mayonnaise (30 ml)
16 oz cream cheese (450 g)
2 tsp Worcestershire sauce (10 ml)
¼ tsp garlic powder (1 ml)
¼ tsp onion juice (1 ml)
⅛ tsp salt (1 ml)
6 oz smoked oysters (170 g)
½ c chopped pecans (120 ml)

Cream mayonnaise and cream cheese together. Add Worcestershire, garlic powder, onion juice, and salt. Mix well. Spread ½-inch (1 cm) thick on waxed paper. Chop oysters and spread over cream cheese. Roll and chill 24 hours. Roll in chopped nuts and serve with crackers or cucumber slices.

Calories per Tbsp: approximately 50.

Crab Meat Canapes

6 oz cream cheese (180 g)
1 Tbsp mayonnaise (15 ml)
7 oz crab meat (210 g)
¼ tsp salad seasoning (1 ml)
½ tsp Worcestershire sauce (3 ml)
Bread rounds or wheat crackers
Paprika

Mix cream cheese, mayonnaise, crab meat, salad seasoning and Worcestershire sauce thoroughly. Refrigerate 1 hour. Spread rounds of bread or wheat crackers with mixture. Sprinkle with paprika and toast in broiler until golden brown.

Makes 1½ cups (360 ml).

Calories per Tbsp: approximately 35.

Chili Rellenos

8 oz canned mild green chilies, drained (250 g)
3 c grated Monterey Jack cheese (720 ml)
1½ c grated Cheddar cheese (360 ml)
2 eggs
2 Tbsp milk (30 ml)
2 Tbsp flour (30 ml)

Cut chilies into strips, discarding seeds if you want a milder taste. Combine chilies, Jack cheese and Cheddar cheese and place in greased 7 × 11-inch (17 × 26 cm) baking dish. Mix eggs, milk and flour well and pour over cheese and chilies. Bake at 375 °F (185 °C) for 35 minutes or until firm. Serve warm, cut in squares.

About 16 appetizers.

Calories per serving: approximately 145.

Cheesy Appetizer

2 c grated sharp Cheddar cheese (480 ml)
½ c butter (120 ml)
1 c all-purpose flour (240 ml)
⅛ tsp cayenne pepper (1 ml)
⅛ tsp salt (1 ml)
36 small stuffed olives or
   36 pitted dates

Blend together cheese and butter. Add flour, cayenne pepper and salt. Work into cheese mixture, forming a dough. Thinly roll out ⅓ of dough on lightly floured board. Cut into 2-inch circles. Wrap around olives or dates. Bake on ungreased baking sheet at 400 °F (200 °C) until lightly browned, about 5 minutes.

Makes 36.

Calories per serving: approximately 85.

Pickled Salmon

2 lb salmon (1 kg)
1½ Tbsp salt (25 ml)
2 Tbsp mixed pickling spices (30 ml)
2 c white wine (480 ml)
2 onions, sliced
4 bay leaves
½ c oil (120 ml)
¾ c white wine vinegar (180 ml)
1 tsp salt (5 ml)
¼ tsp pepper (1 ml)
2 tsp dill weed (10 ml)
Dash liquid pepper seasoning

Cut fish into 1-inch (2.5 cm) pieces. Place in saucepan. Add salt, pickling spices, and wine. Add water, if necessary, to completely cover fish. Bring to a boil. Remove from heat and let stand for 10 minutes. Drain. Layer fish, onions, and bay leaves in a glass bowl. Combine oil, vinegar, salt, pepper, dill weed and liquid pepper. Pour over fish. Refrigerate overnight. Keeps up to 5 days in the refrigerator. Serve on a bed of lettuce as a cold appetizer.

Serves 8.

Calories per serving: approximately 170.

Liver Pate

3 lbs liver (1¼ kg)
1 bay leaf
2 green peppers, whole
1 tsp allspice (5 ml)
1 tsp mace (5 ml)
1 tsp cloves (5 ml)
½ tsp nutmeg (3 ml)
½ tsp pepper (3 ml)
1 tsp salt (5 ml)
2 Tbsp Worcestershire sauce (30 ml)
2 Tbsp lemon juice (30 ml)
½ lb melted butter (240 g)

Boil liver with bay leaf and peppers until cooked throughout. Process in food processor until it is nearly a paste. Add spices, Worcestershire sauce and lemon juice and mix well. Pack in sterilized glasses with melted butter on top to seal. Refrigerate until ready to use. Keeps 1 week.

Calories per Tbsp: approximately 40.

Whatsit

6 English muffins
1 c chopped ripe olives (240 ml)
½ c mayonnaise (120 ml)
½ c grated onion (120 ml)
1½ c grated Cheddar cheese (360 ml)
½ tsp salt (2 ml)
½ tsp curry (2 ml)

Split and toast muffins. Combine olives, mayonnaise, onion, cheese, and seasonings. Spread this filling on muffins and broil for 3 minutes or in microwave for 30 seconds. Cut into quarters to serve.

Calories per serving: approximately 50.

Mellow Yellow Cheese Sticks

2 c flour (480 ml)
1 tsp baking powder (5 ml)
1 tsp salt (5 ml)
¾ c butter (180 ml)
2 eggs
1 Tbsp milk (15 ml)
¼ lb Cheddar cheese, grated (120 g)

Sift flour with baking powder and salt; cut in butter to the size of peas. Add eggs, milk and form dough. Chill dough for 1 hour. Roll chilled dough into a rectangle ¼-inch (½ cm) thick. Sprinkle half the dough with half the grated cheese and cover it with the rest of the dough. Press the edges together to seal the cheese. Fold the dough in half again and roll to original size. Repeat using remainder of cheese. Roll to original size and cut the dough to finger sticks and bake on dry baking sheet at 450°F (230°C) for about 10 minutes or until delicately browned. Cool and store in an airtight container until served. A delicious savory to serve with soup.

Makes 2 dozen.

Calories per serving: approximately 135.

Hot, portable picnics can keep any skier full of energy for the entire day! A picnic basket filled with soups and sandwiches can be kept in the car or lodge to warm up the downhill skier. And backpacks full of tempting treats can keep a cross-country enthusiast going for hours.

A perfect downhill run can cost a skier 8 to 10 calories a minute. Waiting in lift lines costs less than three calories a minute. The number of calories a downhill skier uses depends on ability level...and on the length of the line! Skiers also use up calories keeping warm and often drop a few pounds at the end of the day, regardless of their food intake.

Cross-country skiers may expend up to 1500 calories an hour while racing. In competition, liquids are supplied along the race course, but when skiing for pleasure, backpacks come in handy! Young or inexperienced members of a cross-country team should be given lighter packs...the added weight of a heavier pack will use up even more of their energy.

The best portable foods are lightweight, high calorie dehydrated fruits and trail snacks, soups, and hot liquids carried in thermal containers. Fruits and fruit juices are helpful in replacing lost fluids. The recipes in this chapter are for yummy soups and hot drinks...a perfect accompaniment to sandwiches and breads.

Knapsack Lunches

Rocky Mountain Cheese Soup**
Peasant Bread*
Stuffed Prunes*
Hot Apple Cider

Scandanavian Fish Chowder**
Raw Vegetables
Erik's Oatmeal Crackers*
Beer, Soda

Skier's Tomato Soup**
Longacres Corned Beef Sandwiches**
Helen's Carrot Cookies*
Coffee, Tea or Milk

**In this chapter
*See Index

Batter-up Potato Soup

4 medium potatoes
2 bacon slices, diced
¼ c minced onion (60 ml)
2 Tbsp butter (30 ml)
1 Tbsp chopped parsley (15 ml)
2 tsp salt (10 ml)
½ tsp nutmeg (3 ml)
¼ tsp dry mustard (2 ml)
1 tsp Worcestershire sauce (5 ml)
3 c milk (720 ml)
½ c grated Swiss cheese (120 ml)

Cook potatoes until tender. Saute bacon and onion in butter over low heat. Dice potatoes and add to bacon mixture. Add parsley, nutmeg, mustard, Worcestershire. Stir in milk and heat slowly. Sprinkle with cheese immediately before serving.

Serves 4.

Calories per serving: approximately 300.

Rocky Mountain Cheese Soup

½ c finely chopped carrots (120 ml)
½ c finely chopped celery (120 ml)
¼ c butter (60 ml)
2 Tbsp minced onion (30 ml)
3 Tbsp flour (45 ml)
2 c scalded milk (480 ml)
2 c chicken broth (480 ml)
½ lb Cheddar cheese, shredded (225 g)
2 c small fresh bread cubes (480 ml)
¼ c grated Parmesan cheese (60 ml)

Cook carrots and celery until tender. Drain. Saute onion in double-boiler top placed directly over heat and blend in flour, milk, broth. Bring to a boil stirring until thickened. Place over boiling water and stir in cheese, carrots and celery. Cook for 10 minutes. To serve, place soup in warm bowls and top with bread cubes and Parmesan cheese.

Serves 4.

Calories per serving: approximately 500.

Skier's Tomato Soup

1 clove garlic, minced
1 onion, chopped
1 stalk celery, chopped
1 carrot, chopped
2 tsp oil (10 ml)
2 Tbsp all-purpose flour (30 ml)
1½ c cooked rice (360 ml)
4 tomatoes, chopped
2 tsp salt (10 ml)
1 tsp freshly ground pepper (5 ml)
1 Tbsp sugar (15 ml)
1 tsp basil (5 ml)
1 tsp oregano (5 ml)
4 c hot milk (960 ml)
1 Tbsp butter (15 ml)

Saute garlic, onion, celery and carrot in oil. Add flour and stir, then add rice, tomatoes and seasonings. Bring to a boil. Simmer 5 minutes. Remove from heat and add slowly to the milk and butter. Completely fills a 1-quart, wide-mouth thermos. Serve with homemade bread and cheddar cheese slices.

Serves 4.

Calories per serving: approximately 350.

Scandinavian Fish Chowder

3 c water (720 ml)
3 potatoes, cubed
3 green onions with tops, sliced
1 bay leaf
¾ lb boneless fish fillets or steaks (350 g)
1 c half and half (240 ml)
2 Tbsp flour (30 ml)
1 Tbsp butter (15 ml)
1 tsp salt (5 ml)
¼ tsp pepper (2 ml)
Dash of allspice

In large saucepan, bring to boil water, potatoes, onions and bay leaf. Reduce heat and simmer 20 minutes or until potatoes are tender. Cut fish into cubes and stir in. Cover and simmer 5 minutes. Discard bay leaf. Mix half and half and flour. Add slowly and simmer until soup thickens and fish is done. Stir in butter, salt, pepper and allspice.

Serves 4.

Calories per serving: approximately 280.

Corn and Clam Chowder

4 slices bacon
1½ c finely chopped onions (360 ml)
1 tsp finely chopped garlic
1 potato, cubed
2 c water (480 ml)
18 small hard-shell clams, shucked and
  drained
⅔ c clam liquor (160 ml)
2 c half and half (480 ml)
1½ c cooked corn (360 ml)
1 tsp thyme (5 ml)
¼ tsp freshly ground pepper (2 ml)
2 Tbsp butter, softened (30 ml)
⅛ tsp paprika (1 ml)
2 Tbsp finely chopped parsley (30 ml)
Salt to taste

Fry the bacon in a heavy 2 to 3 quart (3 liter) casserole. When bacon is just soft, stir in the onions and garlic. Stirring frequently, cook for about 5 minutes or until the bacon and onions are a light golden color. Add the potato and water to the sauteed onions. Bring to a boil over high heat. Lower the heat and simmer, partially covered, for about 15 minutes, until potatoes are tender but not falling apart. Add the clams and their liquor, the half and half, corn and thyme, and continue to simmer for 2 or 3 minutes longer; do not allow the chowder to come to a boil. Stir in the pepper and butter, taste for seasoning, adding salt if necessary. Serve at once, sprinkled with paprika and parsley.

Serves 6 - 8.

Calories per serving: approximately 260.

Home Plate Special Zucchini Soup

¼ c butter (60 ml)
2 small green onions, thinly sliced
1 celery stalk, scraped and sliced
1 large carrot, sliced
3 zucchini
3 c chicken broth (720 ml)
Salt and pepper to taste
¼ c grated Parmesan cheese (60 ml)
¼ c sour cream (60 ml)

Melt butter in skillet, stir in onions, celery and carrot and cook until just soft. Cut zucchini into thin slices and add to vegetables along with ¼ c of broth. Cook until zucchini is tender. Add remaining broth, salt and pepper. Simmer for 10 minutes. Chill until ready to serve. Before serving, sprinkle with Parmesan cheese and add a dollop of sour cream.

Serves 4 - 6.

Calories per serving: approximately 120.

Garbanzo Bean Soup

1½ c canned garbanzo beans, drained (360 ml)
1 qt chicken broth (1 liter)
¼ c chopped onion (60 ml)
1 c sliced carrots (240 ml)
1 clove garlic
¼ tsp oregano (1 ml)
½ c chopped Polish sausage (120 ml)
Salt and pepper to taste

Combine garbanzo beans, chicken broth, onion, carrots, garlic, and oregano. Cover and simmer for 25 minutes. Add sausage and continue cooking 5 more minutes. Add salt and pepper to taste and serve.

Serves 3-4.

Calories per serving: approximately 150.

Carrot Dumplings in Chicken Broth

1 c flour (240 ml)
2 tsp baking powder (10 ml)
½ tsp salt (3 ml)
3 Tbsp shortening (45 ml)
½ c milk (120 ml)
¼ c shredded carrot (60 ml)
1 tsp parsley flakes (5 ml)
4 c chicken broth (1 liter)

Mix together flour, baking powder and salt. Cut in shortening until crumbly. Add milk, shredded carrot and parsley flakes. Stir and drop by spoonful into simmering broth. Cover and cook for 15 minutes.

Serves 4.

Calories per serving: approximately 245.

Carrot Soup

2½ c cooked carrots (600 ml)
3 Tbsp butter (45 ml)
1 Tbsp minced onion (15 ml)
3 Tbsp flour (45 ml)
3 c milk (720 ml)
½ c finely chopped celery (120 ml)
Salt and pepper to taste
3 Tbsp chopped parsley (45 ml)

Place cooked carrots in food processor and process until smooth. Melt butter and simmer onion in it. Stir in flour, then milk. Add carrots and celery and simmer 20 minutes. Season to taste with salt and pepper. Garnish with parsley before serving.

Serves 4.

Calories per serving: approximately 115.

Manhattan Vegetable Clam Chowder

3 bacon slices, diced
½ c onions, sliced (120 ml)
1 tsp thyme (5 ml)
3 c potatoes, cubed (720 ml)
½ c diced celery (120 ml)
5 c chicken broth or stock* (1200 ml)
2 tsp salt (10 ml)
¼ tsp pepper (1 ml)
3 tomatoes, diced
1½ c diced carrots (360 ml)
3 c clam nectar (720 ml)
11 oz canned minced clams (325 g)
1 Tbsp chopped parsley (15 ml)

In large kettle, saute bacon and onion until golden brown. Stir in thyme, potatoes, celery, broth, salt and pepper. Simmer for 5 minutes. Add tomatoes, carrots, and clam nectar; simmer for 1 hour. Add clams and parsley to chowder. Continue cooking for a few minutes until heated throughout.

Serves 6 - 8.

Calories per serving: approximately 110.

*Tomato juice may be substituted for up to ¼ of the broth.

Turkey Corn Chowder

4 slices bacon, diced
1 c chopped onion (240 ml)
2 Tbsp flour (30 ml)
4 c cubed potatoes, cooked (1 liter)
2 c turkey broth (480 ml)
2 pkg (10 oz) frozen whole-kernel corn (575 g)
¼ c butter (60 ml)
2½ tsp salt (12 ml)
Freshly ground pepper to taste
2 c cooked turkey, cubed (480 ml)
3 c milk (720 ml)
2 Tbsp chopped parsley (30 ml)

In large kettle, saute bacon and onion. Add flour and stir in well. Add potato and broth and bring to boil. Lower heat and add corn, butter, salt, pepper, turkey and milk. Cook until hot; do not boil. Sprinkle with parsley and serve.

Serves 8 - 10.

Calories per serving: approximately 250.

Burger Soup for Racers

1 lb hamburger (450 g)
1 medium onion, chopped
2 c sliced carrots (480 ml)
1 c peas (240 ml)
2 potatoes, cubed
¼ head cabbage
4 c beef bouillon or broth (960 ml)
2 fresh tomatoes, chopped
Salt and pepper to taste

Brown meat and onion in skillet. Remove excess fat and add remaining ingredients. Bring to a boil, lower heat and simmer for at least 30 minutes or until vegetables are tender.

Makes about 2 quarts of soup or 8 servings.

Calories per serving: approximately 250.

Super Turkey Sandwiches

8 slices crusty French bread or
  4 onion bagels
2 Tbsp butter (30 ml)
2 Tbsp mayonnaise (30 ml)
⅛ tsp curry powder (1 ml)
8 oz cooked turkey, sliced (240 g)
4 slices Provolone or Jarlsberg cheese
1 c bean sprouts (240 ml)

Spread bread with butter and mayonnaise mixed with curry powder. Layer turkey, cheese and sprouts. Wrap well until ready to serve.

Makes 4 sandwiches.

Calories per serving: approximately 450.

Poppy Ham Sandwiches

½ c butter or margarine (120 ml)
¼ c mustard (60 ml)
1 Tbsp poppy seeds (15 ml)
½ c chopped green onion (120 ml)
8 hamburger buns
8 slices Cheddar cheese
16 oz sliced ham (480 g)

Mix together butter, mustard, poppy seeds, and onion; spread ⅛ of the mixture on hamburger buns. Place 1 slice of cheese and 2 oz (60 g) ham slice on each bun. Wrap each in foil and bake in 350°F (175°C) oven or over charcoal coals for 20 minutes. Serve warm or cold.

Makes 8 sandwiches.

Calories per serving: approximately 335.

TFS Sandwiches

8 oz cream cheese, softened (240 g)
¼ c minced onion (60 ml)
¼ c finely chopped green pepper (60 ml)
3 Tbsp chili sauce (45 ml)
5 hard-cooked eggs, finely chopped
½ tsp salt (3 ml)
Dash pepper

Mix all ingredients thoroughly. Refrigerate. Serve with rye bread or toast. This filling can be held in a small wide-mouth thermos. Carry bread along and make sandwiches when you have a long break.

Makes filling for 6 sandwiches.

Calories per serving: approximately 320.

BLT's and Avocado with Russian Dressing

4 slices whole wheat or rye bread
2 tsp butter (10 ml)
2 Tbsp Russian dressing (30 ml)
1 medium tomato, thinly sliced
8 slices bacon, cooked crisp and drained
1 small avocado
2 leaves crisp romaine lettuce

Spread bread with butter and dressing. Arrange tomato and bacon on 2 slices of bread, then cover with 2 remaining slices. Pack romaine and avocado separately to tuck into sandwiches before eating. It is best to leave avocado whole and then just peel and slice right before placing in the sandwich.

Makes 2 sandwiches.

Calories per serving: approximately 500.

Bunsteads

1 c Cheddar cheese, cubed (240 ml)
7 oz canned flaked tuna (210 g)
3 hard-cooked eggs, chopped
2 Tbsp chopped green pepper (30 ml)
2 Tbsp chopped sweet pickle (30 ml)
2 Tbsp chopped onion (30 ml)
⅓ c mayonnaise (80 ml)
2 Tbsp chopped ripe olives (30 ml)
6 sandwich buns

Mix cheese, tuna, eggs, green pepper, pickle, onion, mayonnaise and olives together until well blended. Divide in 6 portions and spread on sandwich buns. Wrap each in foil. Refrigerate until ready to bake. Bake at 350°F (175°) for 30 minutes. If desired, sandwiches may be eaten cold.

Makes 6 sandwiches.

Calories per serving: approximately 425.

Cheese Melts

4 English muffins, split
2 c grated Cheddar cheese (480 ml)
⅓ c sliced green onion (80 ml)
⅓ c mayonnaise (80 ml)
1 tsp curry powder (5 ml)
2 tomatoes, sliced

Toast English muffins. Combine cheese, onion, mayonnaise, and curry powder. Spread on muffins. Broil until cheese melts. Top with tomato slices and serve.

Makes 4 open-faced sandwiches.

Calories per serving: approximately 430.

Hit-and-Run Cheese Egg Sandwich

4 hard-cooked eggs
¼ c mayonnaise (60 ml)
2 Tbsp sweet pickle relish (30 ml)
2 Tbsp chopped green onion (30 ml)
1 Tbsp prepared mustard (15 ml)
6 slices whole wheat bread, toasted
4 oz Mozzarella cheese, sliced (115 g)
1 tomato, sliced

Combine eggs, mayonnaise, relish, onion and mustard. Spread on 6 slices whole wheat or variety bread. Broil about 3 minutes. Top each sandwich with cheese slice and tomato slices. Return to broiler untii cheese melts.

Makes 6 open-faced sandwiches.

Calories per serving: approximately 380.

Peanut Butter Sandwich Filling #1

½ c chopped apple (120 ml)
¼ c honey (60 ml)
½ c peanut butter (120 ml)

Mix together apple, honey and peanut butter. Spread on whole wheat crackers, celery sticks, or toasted English muffins.

Makes 1 cup filling.

Calories per cup: approximately 540.

Peanut Butter Sandwich Filling #2

½ c chunky peanut butter (120 ml)
¼ c chopped dates (60 ml)
1 to 2 Tbsp lemon juice (30 ml)

Blend together and use as a spread for sandwiches, crackers or slices of raw vegetables.

Makes ⅔ cup filling.

Calories per recipe: approximately 360.

Peanut Butter and Carrot Sandwiches

½ c peanut butter (120 ml)
2 medium carrots, shredded (75 ml)
¼ c plain yogurt (60 ml)
2 Tbsp honey (30 ml)
8 slices whole wheat bread

Mix together peanut butter, carrots, yogurt and honey. Spread on bread. This is delicious on zucchini bread as well as on nut breads.

Makes 4 sandwiches.

Calories per serving: approximately 270.

Double Decker Surprise

¼ lb bologna or ham, minced (120 g)
4 oz processed American cheese, diced (120 g)
1 small onion, diced
¼ c pickle relish (60 ml)
¼ c mayonnaise (60 ml)
¼ tsp salt (1 ml)
9 slices whole grain bread
3 Tbsp butter, softened
Lettuce
Tomato slices

Mix meat, cheese, onion, relish, mayonnaise and salt. For each sandwich, spread 2 slices of bread with butter, then approximately ¼ cup meat mixture. Butter both sides of another slice of bread. Stack with double buttered bread in the middle, adding the lettuce and tomato.

Makes 3 sandwiches.

Calories per serving: approximately 600.

Longacres' Corned Beef Sandwiches

8 slices of rye bread
Butter
Prepared horseradish
Prepared mustard
¾ lb cooked lean corned beef, sliced (360 g)
1 onion, paper thin slices
4 slices Swiss cheese

Spread 4 slices of bread with butter. Spread the remaining slices with horseradish and mustard; pile on the corned beef, onion and cheese. Cover with buttered slices.

Makes 4 sandwiches.

Calories per serving: approximately 270.

Touchdown Sandwiches

8-oz cream cheese (225 g)
8¼-oz canned crushed pineapple, drained
  (240 g)
12 slices day-old bread
6 slices ham or luncheon meat
3 eggs, slightly beaten
½ c milk (120 ml)
¼ c margarine (60 ml)

Beat cream cheese until fluffy; stir in pineapple. Spread 6 slices of bread generously with the mixture. Top with meat, then with the remaining bread slices. Cut each sandwich in half diagonally. Mix eggs and milk. Melt half the margarine in large skillet. Dip both sides of sandwich in egg mixture. Saute in hot margarine, turning and adding more margarine, if needed, for 5 minutes, or until lightly browned on both sides. Serve hot.

Makes 6 sandwiches.

Calories per serving: approximately 420.

Competition in tennis involves long, exhausting work...often outside in hot weather. Crisp salads and vegetables are cool, refreshing pick-ups after the game and a colorful accompaniment to meals.

This stop and start sport uses very few calories a minute, but when it's time to move, the player needs immense energy and ability to concentrate. Tennis players make errors when hungry and dehydrated...giving a cheap shot to the other side! The answer is three meals a day, with emphasis on carbohydrate for energy and increased fluid intake to prevent dehydration.

The following salads and vegetable dishes are perfect as delectable one-dish lunches on a sunny afternoon...or an eye-pleasing part of a perfect menu.

After the Match Luncheons

Thin Slices of Prosciutto & Melon
Salade Nicoise**
Erik's Oatmeal Crackers*
Iced Fruit Juices

Aunt Erva's Exotic Chicken Salad**
Broiled Tomatoes with Dill Sauce**
Whole Wheat Biscuits*
Pineapple Smash*

Fresh Fruit Salad**
Banana Dressing**
Country Fair Scones*
Cheese Tray
Iced Tea or Coffee

Recipes from tennis players:

Trish Bostrom's Eggplant & Cheese Casserole**
  Nationally ranked doubles player

Bill Feinberg's Flank Steak Marinade*
  Nationally ranked table tennis champion

**In this chapter
*See Index

Italian-style Mixed Green Salad

1 large head romaine
2 tomatoes
1 small zucchini
¾ c cooked garbanzo beans (180 ml)
⅓ c wine vinegar
⅓ c olive oil (80 ml)
1 tsp salt (5 ml)
¼ tsp pepper (1 ml)
⅛ tsp garlic powder (1 ml)
⅛ tsp tarragon (1 ml)
5 oz Jack cheese, cut into cubes (150 g)
2 oz Italian salami, thinly sliced (60 g)

Wash romaine and tear into bite-size pieces. Cut tomatoes into wedges; slice zucchini and add to lettuce along with the drained garbanzo beans. Combine vinegar, oil, salt, pepper, garlic powder and tarragon in a jar. Shake well and pour over salad. Toss lightly until just blended. Top with cheese and thinly sliced salami.

Serves 8.

Calories per serving: approximately 160.

Garden Green Salad

1 head red leaf lettuce
2 avocados
2 carrots
1 c bean sprouts (240 ml)
Dill Dressing*
Croutons

Wash lettuce and tear into bite-size pieces. Peel avocados and carrots and chop. Mix with sprouts and lettuce. Just before serving, top with Dill Dressing; sprinkle with croutons. Toss gently with dressing to coat the salad evenly.

Serves 8.

Calories per serving: approximately 150.

*See index

Romaine Citrus Salad

½ tsp grated orange peel (3 ml)
¼ c orange juice (60 ml)
½ c salad oil (120 ml)
1 Tbsp lemon juice (15 ml)
2 Tbsp sugar (30 ml)
2 Tbsp red wine vinegar (30 ml)
¼ tsp salt (1 ml)
3 c romaine, washed and crisp (720 ml)
1 small cucumber, thinly sliced
1 avocado, sliced
11-oz mandarin oranges, drained (330 g)
1 small onion, sliced in rings

Combine orange peel, orange juice, salad oil, lemon juice, sugar, vinegar and salt in a jar. Cover and shake well. Chill. Place lettuce, cucumber, avocado, oranges and onion in salad bowl. Add chilled dressing and toss to mix.

Serves 8.

Calories per serving: approximately 180.

Artichoke Salad

1 head leaf lettuce
2 tomatoes
½ c grated Jack cheese (120 ml)
6-oz black olives (180 g)
Cucumber Dressing*
6-oz marinated artichoke hearts (180 g)

Wash lettuce and tear into bite-size pieces. Seed and chop tomatoes and add to lettuce with grated Jack cheese. Slice the black olives, add with dressing to salad and gently toss. Cut artichoke hearts in quarters and garnish just before serving.

Serves 8.

Calories per serving: approximately 150.

*See index.

Spinach Salad

1 head lettuce
1 bunch spinach
1 Tbsp butter (15 ml)
½ c sesame seeds (120 ml)
¼ c Parmesan cheese (60 ml)
4 slices cooked bacon, crumbled
1 c sour cream (240 ml)
1 Tbsp white vinegar (15 ml)
1 Tbsp sugar (15 ml)
¼ c chopped green pepper (60 ml)
1 small green onion, sliced
½ tsp salt (3 ml)
¼ tsp garlic salt (1 ml)

Break lettuce into bite-size chunks; tear spinach leaves and place in salad bowl with lettuce. Melt butter in small pan, and lightly brown sesame seeds. Cool, add Parmesan cheese and bacon bits. Add to greens. Combine sour cream, vinegar, sugar, green pepper, onion, salt and garlic salt. When ready to serve, pour over greens, toss lightly.

Serves 8-10.

Calories per serving: approximately 100.

Oasis Salad

1 head of bibb lettuce, washed and chilled
1 ripe avocado
½ c creamy Italian salad dressing (120 ml)
¼ c sunflower seeds (60 ml)

Tear lettuce into bite-sized pieces. Peel avocado and slice lengthwise into pieces. Pour salad dressing over lettuce and avocado slices and toss. Sprinkle sunflower seeds on top and serve on chilled salad plates.

Serves 4.

Calories per serving: approximately 170.

Pot Luck Dinner Overnight Salad

1 head iceberg lettuce, torn in pieces
8 slices bacon, fried and crumbled
1 c celery, sliced (240 ml)
½ c green pepper, diced (120 ml)
1 onion, diced
4 hard-cooked eggs, sliced
½ c grated cheese (120 ml)
10-oz frozen peas, separated, but not thawed
   (285 g)
2 c mayonnaise (480 ml)
2 Tbsp sugar (30 ml)

In a deep bowl put half of the lettuce, then arrange in layers the bacon, celery, green peppers, onion, eggs, cheese and peas. Top with the remaining lettuce. Blend together the mayonnaise and sugar and spread over top of salad like icing. Cover bowl and refrigerate for 12 hours. Serve by slicing down through all the layers.

Serves 8 - 12.

Calories per serving: approximately 550.

Creamy Coleslaw

1 small Chinese cabbage, thinly sliced
1 small green pepper, sliced
½ c mayonnaise (120 ml)
½ c sour cream (120 ml)
2 tsp lemon juice (10 ml)
½ tsp salt (3 ml)
½ tsp pepper (3 ml)
¼ tsp dry mustard (1 ml)

Place cabbage and green pepper in bowl. Mix mayonnaise, sour cream, lemon juice, salt, pepper and mustard. Add to cabbage and peppers. Mix well.

Serves 4 - 6.

Calories per serving: approximately 250.

Potato Salad

8 large potatoes
1 pkg (¾-oz) Italian salad dressing mix (22 g)
¼ c chopped green onion (60 ml)
½ c chopped celery (120 ml)
¼ c chopped green pepper (60 ml)
¾ c white wine (180 ml) or
  ½ c vinegar (120 ml)
⅓ c salad oil (80 ml)
1 to 2 Tbsp sugar (15 to 30 ml)

Cook unpeeled potatoes in boiling water until tender. Cool slightly and remove peel. Cut into pieces, sprinkle with salad dressing mix and add all other ingredients while potatoes are still warm. Allow to stand overnight in the refrigerator. Serve warm or cold.

Serves 6 - 8.

Calories per serving: approximately 180.

Double Tuna Salad

⅔ c brown rice (160 ml)
7-oz can chunk tuna, drained and broken into
  chunks (210 g)
1 c shredded carrot (240 ml)
1 c diced celery (240 ml)
2 Tbsp chopped onion (30 ml)
½ c mayonnaise (120 ml)
2 tsp lemon juice (10 ml)
¼ tsp Worcestershire sauce (2 ml)
¼ tsp salt (2 ml)
¼ tsp dried mixed salad herbs (2 ml)
6 lettuce leaves

Cook rice, rinse with cold water and drain. Add tuna, carrot, celery and onion; chill. Before serving, add dressing made of mayonnaise, lemon juice, Worcestershire sauce, salt and herbs. Toss lightly and serve on lettuce leaves, if desired.

Serves 4 - 6.

Calories per serving: approximately 300.

Grand Prix Mushroom Salad

1 lb fresh mushrooms (450 g)
¼ c chopped chives (60 ml)
⅓ c lemon juice (80 ml)
⅓ c olive oil (80 ml)
1 tsp sugar (5 ml)
1 tsp salt (5 ml)
½ tsp pepper (3 ml)
½ tsp basil (optional) (3 ml)

Clean and slice mushrooms. Add chives, lemon juice, oil, sugar, salt, pepper and basil. Mix together and refrigerate overnight. Serve on lettuce leaves.

Serves 4 - 6.

Calories per serving: approximately 85.

Carrot and Peanut Salad

4 large carrots, shredded
½ c mayonnaise (120 ml)
1 c salted peanuts, chopped (240 ml)
1 tsp grated onion (5 ml)
Paprika

Combine and toss lightly. Chill before serving.

Serves 4 - 5.

Calories per serving: approximately 500.

Aunt Erva's Exotic Chicken Salad

1½ lb cooked chicken or turkey (700 g)
8-oz water chestnuts, sliced (225 g)
1 lb seedless green grapes, halved (450 g)
⅓ c diced celery (80 ml)
⅓ c toasted almonds (80 ml)
8 crisp lettuce leaves
1½ c mayonnaise (360 ml)
1 Tbsp curry (15 ml)
1 Tbsp soy sauce (15 ml)
1 Tbsp lemon juice (15 ml)

Cut chicken into bite-size pieces. Place chicken, water chestnuts, grapes, celery and almonds in a bowl and chill. Place lettuce leaves on chilled salad plates. Combine mayonnaise, curry, soy sauce and lemon juice. Mix with chicken mixture. Place on lettuce just before serving.

Serves 8.

Calories per serving: approximately 300.

Salade Nicoise

6-oz can tuna, drained (180 g)
8 anchovy fillets
2 hard-cooked eggs, quartered
2 cooked potatoes, sliced
4 tomatoes
½ medium head of lettuce
½ Spanish onion, sliced
1 green pepper, sliced
8 radishes
4 stalks celery, sliced
8 ripe olives

Dressing

2 Tbsp wine vinegar or lemon juice (30 ml)
⅓ c olive oil (80 ml)
¼ tsp dry mustard (1 ml)
¼ tsp sugar (1 ml)
¼ tsp basil (1 ml)
Salt and pepper

Place drained tuna in bottom of serving dish with anchovies, eggs, potatoes, tomatoes, and lettuce. Arrange sliced onion, green pepper, radishes, celery and olives on top. Mix together vinegar, olive oil, dry mustard, sugar and basil and pour over salad. Add salt and pepper to taste.

Serves 4 - 6.

Calories per serving: approximately 350.

Guacamole Salad

1 clove garlic
2 avocados
2 Tbsp fresh lemon juice (30 ml)
3 tomatoes
2 Tbsp chopped onion (30 ml)
¼ c mayonnaise (60 ml)
Dash of Tabasco
½ tsp salt (3 ml)
½ tsp freshly ground pepper (3 ml)
2 tsp chili powder (10 ml)
Tortilla chips or lettuce

Mash garlic and avocado and add lemon juice. Seed and chop tomato. Add to avocados along with onion, mayonnaise, Tabasco, salt and pepper. Add chili powder if a spicy salad is desired. Serve as a dip with corn tortilla chips or on a bed of shredded lettuce.

Serves 4.

Calories per serving: approximately 240.

Melody Salad

1 c diced apple (240 ml)
½ c diced dill pickle (120 ml)
½ c diced celery (120 ml)
½ c diced hard-cooked egg (120 ml)
½ c diced cooked meat (120 ml)
½ c tuna, drained (120 ml)
½ c chopped green onion (120 ml)
½ c mayonnaise (120 ml)
1 tsp dry mustard (5 ml)
2 tsp lemon juice (10 ml)
Salt
Pepper

Place apple, pickle, celery, egg, meat, tuna, and green onion in a bowl. Combine mayonnaise, mustard and lemon juice and add enough to the salad to moisten it. Season with salt and pepper to taste and serve.

Serves 4.

Calories per serving: approximately 430.

Fresh Fruit Salad

2 bananas
1 avocado
1 orange
1 apple
1 c seedless green grapes (240 ml)
1 c strawberries, hulled (240 ml)
½ c Banana* or Celery Seed Dressing*

Peel and slice bananas, avocado, and orange. Core apple and coarsely chop and add to bananas along with grapes and strawberries. Chill until ready to serve. Just before serving, blend in ½ c of Banana Dressing or Celery Seed Dressing.

Serves 6.

Calories per serving: approximately 160.

*See index.

Olympic Vegetable Salad

1 c bulgur wheat (240 ml)
1 c boiling water (240 ml)
½ c lemon juice (120 ml)
2 tsp salt (10 ml)
¼ tsp freshly ground pepper (1 ml)
1 cucumber, sliced
2 tomatoes, diced
1 c sliced green onions (240 ml)
½ c fresh parsley (120 ml)
¼ c chopped fresh mint leaves (60 ml)
1 head romaine lettuce, washed and drained

Place bulgur in a large mixing bowl and pour boiling water over it; let stand 10 minutes and then stir. Place lemon juice, oil, salt and pepper in a jar; cover and shake well. Pour dressing over bulgur, add remaining ingredients except lettuce and toss. Cover and chill. To serve, place in scoops on romaine.

Serves 8.

Calories per serving: approximately 185.

Fruit and Vegetable Salad

2 bananas, sliced
1 large apple, chopped
1 large carrot, grated
⅔ c raisins (160 ml)
½ c sunflower seeds (120 ml)
2 c alfalfa sprouts (480 ml)
⅓ c mayonnaise (80 ml)
2 Tbsp honey (30 ml)

Place bananas, apple, carrots, raisins, sunflower seeds and alfalfa sprouts in a large bowl. Mix mayonnaise and honey and pour over salad just before serving. Toss gently until well mixed.

Serves 6.

Calories per serving: approximately 300.

Banana Dressing

½ c mayonnaise (120 ml)
½ c yogurt (120 ml)
2 Tbsp honey (30 ml)
2 Tbsp lemon juice (30 ml)
½ tsp cinnamon (3 ml)
2 bananas, mashed

Blend ingredients well. Chill. Serve over fruit salads. This dressing keeps for only one day.

Makes about 2 cups.

Calories per Tbsp: approximately 45.

Mexican Salad Dressing

2 Tbsp sugar (30 ml)
⅔ c oil (160 ml)
¼ c Worcestershire sauce (60 ml)
¼ c chili sauce (60 ml)
⅔ c catsup (160 ml)
⅓ c wine vinegar (80 ml)
1 tsp powdered oregano (5 ml)
½ tsp salt (3 ml)
1 clove garlic, quartered

Shake all ingredients together. Let stand at least 1 hour to blend flavors. Pour over mixed greens or vegetable salad.

Makes about 2 cups.

Calories per Tbsp: approximately 50.

Dill Dressing

½ c mayonnaise (120 ml)
1 c yogurt (240 ml)
1 Tbsp dill weed (15 ml)
½ tsp salt (3 ml)
¼ tsp pepper (1 ml)

Combine ingredients, blending well. Chill. Serve over tossed green salad or cold left-over vegetables such as green beans or peas.

Makes 1½ cups.

Calories per Tbsp: approximately 50.

Cucumber Dressing

½ c mayonnaise (120 ml)
½ c plain yogurt (120 ml)
½ c chopped, seeded cucumber (120 ml)
¼ tsp onion powder (1 ml)
¼ tsp garlic powder (1 ml)
½ tsp black pepper (1 ml)

Blend ingredients well. Chill. Serve with tossed green salad.

Makes 1½ cups.

Calories per Tbsp: approximately 45.

Celery Seed Dressing

⅓ c light corn syrup (80 ml)
¼ c vinegar (60 ml)
¼ c sugar (60 ml)
1½ tsp celery seed (7 ml)
1 tsp dry mustard (5 ml)
1 tsp salt (5 ml)
Freshly ground pepper
1 thinly sliced onion
1 c oil (240 ml)

Place all ingredients, except oil, in blender. Blend, then slowly add oil one-fourth at a time. Serve with coleslaw or fruit slaw.

Makes 1½ cups.

Calories per Tbsp: approximately 100.

Avocado Salad Mold

3-oz lime gelatin (90 g)
1 Tbsp fresh lemon juice (15 ml)
1 c boiling water (240 ml)
1 Tbsp grated onion (15 ml)
2 Tbsp chopped green pepper (30 ml)
½ c diced celery (120 ml)
2 medium diced avocados
½ c mayonnaise (120 ml)
½ c whipping cream (120 ml)
1 Tbsp sugar (15 ml)

Place gelatin in a bowl and add lemon juice and boiling water; stir until gelatin is dissolved. Add onion, green pepper, celery, avocados and mayonnaise. Whip cream; add sugar and fold into gelatin mixture. Pour into mold and allow to set for at least two hours in refrigerator.

Serves 6.

Calories per serving: approximately 400.

Cranberry Relish Mold

3-oz pkg lemon flavored gelatin (90 g)
1 c boiling water (240 ml)
10-oz can cranberry-orange relish (300 g)
1 c crushed pineapple, undrained (240 ml)
1 unpared, red apple, chopped
½ c chopped celery (120 ml)
½ c chopped nuts (120 ml)
1 tsp cinnamon (5 ml)
½ tsp nutmeg (3 ml)

Dissolve gelatin in boiling water. Stir in relish, pineapple, apple, celery, nuts, cinnamon and nutmeg. Pour into 1 qt (1 liter) mold. Chill until set. Serve on lettuce or fresh spinach leaves.

Serves 6 - 8.

Calories per serving: approximately 150.

Molded Apple-Cinnamon Salad

3-oz lemon-flavored gelatin (90 g)
⅓ c cinnamon candies (80 ml)
1 c boiling water (240 ml)
1½ c applesauce (360 ml)
¼ c mayonnaise (60 ml)
½ c chopped nuts (120 ml)
¼ c diced celery (60 ml)
4-oz cream cheese (120 g)

Dissolve gelatin and candies in boiling water; add applesauce and pour half into 1 qt (1 liter) mold and chill until set. Combine mayonnaise, nuts, celery and cream cheese and spoon carefully over set gelatin. Top with remaining gelatin and chill until firm.

Serves 6.

Calories per serving: approximately 320.

Tomato-Zucchini Scallop

2 small zucchini squash, sliced
1 medium onion, thinly sliced
½ c cherry tomatoes, cut in half (120 ml)
1 c plain croutons (240 ml)
1 tsp salt (5 ml)
¼ tsp pepper (1 ml)
1 c grated Cheddar cheese (240 ml)
1 Tbsp sesame seeds, toasted (15 ml)
2 Tbsp parsley (30 ml)

In a 1½ qt (1½ liter) casserole, layer half of the zucchini, onion, tomatoes and croutons. Season with half the salt and dash of pepper. Repeat layers. Cover and bake at 350°F (175°C) for 30 minutes. Uncover and sprinkle with cheese, sesame seeds and parsley. Return to oven for 10 minutes.

Serves 6.

Calories per serving: approximately 130.

Broiled Tomatoes with Dill Sauce

½ c sour cream (120 ml)
¼ c mayonnaise (60 ml)
2 Tbsp chopped onion (30 ml)
¼ tsp dill weed (1 ml)
¼ tsp salt (1 ml)
3 large, firm, ripe tomatoes
Salt and pepper
Butter

Combine sour cream, mayonnaise, onion, dill weed and salt. Mix well. Cut tomatoes in half crosswise, season with salt and pepper and dot with butter. Broil, cut side up, 5 minutes or until heated through. Spoon sauce over tomatoes.

Serves 6.

Calories per serving: approximately 140.

Deviled Brussels Sprouts

2 lb Brussels sprouts (1 kg)
⅓ c butter (80 ml)
2 tsp prepared mustard (10 ml)
1 tsp Worcestershire sauce (5 ml)
1 Tbsp chili sauce (15 ml)
Salt and pepper

Wash sprouts and trim off stem end, if necessary. Cut an "X" in stem end and place sprouts in pan with water. Cook sprouts until tender; drain. Melt butter in a small saucepan. Add remaining ingredients and stir until smooth. Pour over sprouts and serve.

Serves 8.

Calories per serving: approximately 85.

Trish Bostrom's Eggplant and Cheese Casserole

1 medium-size eggplant, peeled and cubed
Boiling water
½ c milk (120 ml)
2 slices whole wheat bread
2 eggs, beaten
1 c grated Cheddar cheese (240 ml)

Preheat oven to 350°F (175°C). Put the eggplant pieces in a saucepan with water to cover. Cover and simmer until tender, about 15 minutes. Drain and mash eggplant. Meanwhile, pour milk over bread and cover. Let soak 5 minutes. Squeeze excess milk from bread. Pull apart and add to eggplant; mix. Add eggs and cheese and mix. Pour into an oiled casserole and bake 1 hour, or until set and lightly browned on top.

Serves 6.

Calories per serving: approximately 250.

Trish Bostrom is a nationally ranked doubles player.

California Spoon Bread

16-oz can cream-style corn (450 g)
¾ c milk (180 ml)
¼ c oil (60 ml)
2 eggs
1 c yellow cornmeal (240 ml)
½ tsp baking soda (3 ml)
1 tsp salt (5 ml)
¼ c chopped green pepper (60 ml)
¼ c chopped green onion (60 ml)
1½ c grated Cheddar cheese (360 ml)

Mix together corn, milk, oil and eggs. Add cornmeal, baking soda and salt and blend until well mixed. Pour half the batter into a greased 9 × 9-inch (23 × 23 cm) pan. Sprinkle with green pepper, onion and half of the cheese. Spread remaining batter on top and sprinkle with remaining cheese. Bake at 400°F (200°C) for 45 minutes or until set. Remove from oven and cool for 5 minutes before serving. This is an excellent accompaniment to baked salmon or roasted meats.

Serves 9.

Calories per serving: approximately 225.

Carrot Delight

2 c carrots, cooked (480 ml)
¼ c minced onion (60 ml)
2 c frozen green peas (480 ml)
1 c milk (240 ml)
1 tsp salt (5 ml)
1 tsp pepper (5 ml)
3 eggs, beaten
⅓ c soft butter (80 ml)
½ c cracker crumbs (120 ml)
½ c sharp Cheddar cheese, grated (120 ml)

In a casserole, combine carrots, onion and peas. Mix together milk, salt, pepper, eggs and butter. Pour over vegetables. Combine cracker crumbs and cheese and place on top. Bake at 350°F (175°C) for 45 minutes or until done.

Serves 8.

Calories per serving: approximately 170.

Sweet and Sour Zucchini Strips

1 large onion, chopped
1 Tbsp oil (15 ml)
1½ lb small zucchini, cut in strips (700 g)
1 tsp paprika (5 ml)
1 Tbsp butter (15 ml)
1 Tbsp flour (15 ml)
¼ c cider vinegar (60 ml)
¼ tsp dill weed (2 ml)
1 Tbsp sugar (15 ml)
½ tsp salt (3 ml)

Saute onion in oil. Cook zucchini in boiling water for 3 minutes, drain, and add to onion. Sprinkle with paprika. Blend butter and flour together and add to zucchini with vinegar, dill weed, sugar and salt. Cover and cook 5 minutes or until zucchini is tender but still crisp and crunchy.

Serves 4.

Calories per serving: approximately 130.

Scalloped Corn

1 c bread crumbs (240 ml)
¼ c butter (60 ml)
½ green pepper, chopped (120 ml)
½ medium onion, chopped (120 ml)
2 Tbsp flour (30 ml)
1 tsp salt (5 ml)
¼ tsp dry mustard (1 ml)
1 c milk (240 ml)
1 egg, beaten
16-oz can corn (450 g)

Brown bread crumbs in 2 Tbsp (30 ml) butter. Set aside. Cook green pepper and onion slowly in remaining 2 Tbsp butter for 5 minutes. Add flour, salt and mustard, mixing well. Add milk and cook until thick. Add half the bread crumbs, egg and corn and pour into greased 9 × 9-inch (23 × 23 cm) baking dish. Cover with remaining bread crumbs. Bake at 400°F (200°C) for 20 minutes.

Serves 6.

Calories per serving: approximately 290.

Oriental Green Beans

20-oz frozen French-cut green beans (570 g)
2 Tbsp butter (30 ml)
2 Tbsp minced onion (30 ml)
1 c fresh bean sprouts (240 ml)
12-oz can sliced water chestnuts, drained
   (360 g)
10½-oz can condensed cream of chicken
   soup (315 g)
1 c milk (240 ml)
½ c shredded sharp Cheddar cheese (120 ml)
3½-oz can French-fried onions (100 g)

Cook green beans, drain and set aside. Melt butter in fry pan, add onion, bean sprouts and sliced chestnuts; cover and cook for 3 minutes. Place half of the beans in a buttered 2½ qt (2 liter) casserole; spread with half the bean sprout mixture. Combine soup with milk and spoon half of it over the vegetables. Repeat layers. Top with shredded cheese. Bake uncovered at 400°F (200°C) for 25 minutes. Remove from oven and cover with onion rings. Return to oven for 5 minutes.

Serves 8.

Calories per serving: approximately 180.

Green Beans au Gratin

¼ c butter (60 ml)
¼ c flour (60 ml)
1 tsp salt (5 ml)
⅛ tsp dry mustard (1 ml)
1½ c milk (360 ml)
½ c Cheddar cheese, grated (120 ml)
10½-oz frozen green beans (315 g)
2 Tbsp Parmesan cheese, grated (30 ml)
Paprika

Melt butter in saucepan; add flour, salt and mustard and cook until bubbly. Add milk and cook until thickened, stirring occasionally. Add Cheddar cheese and stir until melted. Add green beans and pour into buttered casserole, sprinkle with grated Parmesan cheese and paprika. Bake at 375°F (185°C) for 25-30 minutes.

Serves 6.

Calories per serving: approximatley 200.

Fresh Asparagus Casserole

2 lb fresh asparagus, cooked (1 kg)
2-oz pimentos, sliced (60 g)
6 hard-cooked eggs, sliced
8 oz sharp Cheddar cheese, grated (240 g)
½ c butter or margarine (120 ml)
½ c flour (120 ml)
13½-oz evaporated milk (340 ml)
1⅓ c milk (320 ml)
1 tsp salt (5 ml)
½ c almonds (120 ml)

Place ½ the asparagus in a greased casserole dish. Add half the pimentos and half the sliced eggs. Sprinkle with half of the cheese. Melt butter in a saucepan and add flour. Mix well and slowly add evaporated milk, milk and salt. Stirring constantly, bring to a boil. Pour half over asparagus. Repeat layers; sprinkle with almonds. Bake at 350°F (175°C) for 20 minutes or until hot and bubbly.

Serves 8-12.

Calories per serving: approximately 340.

Cauliflower au Gratin

10-oz pkg frozen cauliflower (300 g)
1 Tbsp butter (15 ml)
1 Tbsp all-purpose flour (15 ml)
¼ tsp salt (1 ml)
¼ tsp pepper (1 ml)
1 tsp dry mustard (5 ml)
1 c milk (240 ml)
1 c grated processed American cheese
  (240 ml)
¼ c wheat germ (60 ml)
¼ c bran flake cereal (60 ml)
1 tsp melted butter (5 ml)
¼ tsp salt (1 ml)
¼ tsp sage (1 ml)
¼ tsp dry mustard (1 ml)

Thaw cauliflower and spread in bottom of ungreased 1-quart (1 liter) casserole. Prepare white sauce by melting butter in fry pan. Blend in flour and seasonings, stir until smooth. Stir in milk and bring to boil; add grated cheese and stir until melted. Pour over vegetables. Combine the remaining ingredients for topping and sprinkle over the sauce. Bake uncovered at 325°F (165°C) for 15 minutes.

Serves 4.

Calories per serving: approximately 200.

Acorn Squash with Pecans

2 medium acorn squash
½ c soft butter (120 ml)
2 Tbsp brown sugar (30 ml)
½ tsp salt (2 ml)
½ tsp cinnamon (2 ml)
1 Tbsp grated orange peel (15 ml)
Juice of 1 orange
½ c coarsely chopped pecans (120 ml)
Water

Cut squash in half lengthwise; scoop out seeds. Cream butter, brown sugar, salt, cinnamon and orange peel. Stir in orange juice and add in nuts. Pour ½-inch (1 cm) of water in large baking pan and place squash cut side up in it. Divide butter mixture evenly and place in squash cavities. Cover pan with foil and bake at 375°F (185°C) for 40 minutes. Uncover and continue baking for 30 more minutes or until tender.

Serves 4.

Calories per serving: approximately 260.

Sherried Sweet Potato Casserole

3 c cooked, sliced sweet potato (720 ml)
¼ c butter (60 ml)
¼ c sherry (60 ml)
¼ c orange juice (60 ml)
¼ tsp fresh grated orange peel (2 ml)
¼ tsp salt (2 ml)
⅛ tsp pepper (1 ml)
¼ c brown sugar (60 ml)

Place sweet potatoes in a buttered 2 quart (2 liter) casserole. In a saucepan, combine butter, sherry, orange juice, orange peel, salt and pepper; heat until butter is melted and sauce is warm. Pour over sweet potatoes. Bake at 350°F (175°C) for 20 minutes. Sprinkle brown sugar on potatoes and return to oven for 10 more minutes.

Serves 6.

Calories per serving: approximately 260.

Potato-Cheese Patties

3 c mashed potatoes (720 ml)
½ c shredded cheese, packed (120 ml)
1 tsp salt (5 ml)
¼ tsp pepper (1 ml)
½ c bran flakes (120 ml)
½ c wheat germ (120 ml)
2 Tbsp dried parsley (30 ml)
1 Tbsp onion salt (15 ml)

Combine potatoes, cheese, salt and pepper and form into patties. Combine bran flakes, wheat germ, parsley and salt and dip patties in mixture. Place on greased cookie sheet and bake at 320°F (165°C) for 20 to 25 minutes or until brown.

Serves 6.

Calories per serving: approximately 110.

Hopping John

¼ c rice, uncooked (60 ml)
1 c ham broth (240 ml)
2 c canned blackeyed peas (480 ml)
⅓ c chopped onion (80 ml)
Salt and pepper
1 Tbsp butter (15 ml)
½ c chopped cooked ham (120 ml)
½ green pepper, diced (120 ml)
10½-oz condensed cream of mushroom soup (300 g)

Cook rice in ham broth until tender (about 20 minutes). Combine rice and remaining broth with the rest of ingredients. Place in 2-qt (2 liter) covered casserole and bake at 350°F (175°C) for 30 minutes.

Serves 4.

Calories per serving: approximately 220.

Darell Corn's Potatoes

2 Tbsp butter (30 ml)
¼ lb fresh mushrooms, sliced (120 g)
2 Tbsp flour (30 ml)
1 c buttermilk (240 ml)
¼ tsp Worcestershire sauce (2 ml)
1 c Cheddar cheese, grated (240 ml)
1 tsp salt (5 ml)
¼ tsp pepper (5 ml)
3 medium potatoes, cooked and sliced
3 hard-cooked eggs, sliced
¼ c toasted sesame seeds (60 ml)

In a saucepan, saute mushrooms in butter. Stir in flour, then buttermilk; continue stirring until thickened. Add Worcestershire sauce, then cheese, salt and pepper. In a 9 × 9-inch (23 × 23 cm) buttered casserole, layer potatoes, eggs and cheese sauce. Top with sesame seeds and bake at 350 °F (175 °C) for 20 minutes.

Serves 4.

Calories per serving: approximately 300.

Darell Corn is the record holder in shot & discus at Seattle Pacific University.

Fiesta Potatoes

3 c frozen hash brown potatoes (720 ml)
10½-oz cream of celery soup (315 g)
½ c sour cream (120 ml)
1 tsp chives or green onions (5 ml)
½ c Cheddar cheese, grated (120 ml)
2 slices bacon, cooked and crumbled

Mix potatoes with soup, sour cream, and onions. Top with cheese and bacon bits. Bake at 350 °F (175 °C) for 45 minutes.

Serves 6.

Calories per serving: approximately 250.

Brown Rice with Mushrooms

¼ c butter (60 ml)
¼ c minced onion (60 ml)
1 c brown rice (240 ml)
2 c chicken broth (480 ml)
½ tsp salt (3 ml)
¼ tsp pepper (1 ml)
8 oz fresh mushrooms, sliced (220 g)

Melt butter in a skillet. Add onion and brown rice. Saute about 5 minutes until onion is limp but not browned. Add broth, salt, pepper and mushrooms. Cover and let simmer for 35 minutes or until rice is tender, adding more water during cooking if necessary.

Serves 4 - 6.

Calories per serving: approximately 180.

Orange Rice with Fresh Parsley

¼ c butter or margarine (60 ml)
1 c rice, uncooked (240 ml)
½ tsp salt (3 ml)
Dash of white pepper
2½ c chicken broth (600 ml)
½ c orange juice (120 ml)
¼ c fresh chopped parsley (60 ml)

Place butter, rice, salt, pepper and broth in casserole. Cover and bake at 350 °F (175 °C) until light and feathery, about 45 minutes. Add orange juice and return to oven for 10 minutes. Taste for seasoning and toss with a fork. Sprinkle with chopped parsley.

Serves 4 - 6.

Calories per serving: approximately 200.

Football requires two nutritional absolutes: adequate fluids on the field and a diet adjusted to the caloric intake of the individual player and his activity on the field. Practice sessions are intense and the player needs huge intakes of both fluids and calories. More medical problems are recorded in football than in any other sport. Many of these injuries are related to heat and exhaustion.

A major nutritional emphasis in football is weight gain. The adolescent player however, often loses weight during pre-season. If weight gain is a goal for the athlete, a realistic range of gain can be agreed upon between the coach, player, and mother (or the supplier of the extra calories needed for the gain). A complete physical is required and careful attention must be given to blood chemistry levels during such a regimen. Since an acceptable rate of gain is 2 pounds per week or less, a good time to think about gaining weight is in the spring before the two-a-day practices begin.

The football game itself does not require large amounts of calories as each player plays only a few total minutes. But the pre-game meal is an important one. This occasion establishes the rapport of the team as well as providing the fuel for this high energy sport. This means that the meal should be satisfying, but not as heavy as has been traditionally established. For nervous stomachs, a nutritious liquid meal is appropriate. The meal should be relatively low in fat, low in protein, and high in carbohydrates. It should be eaten at least 4 hours before the event.

The following recipes are very hearty dinners that will help keep weight gain easy. Eaten in smaller quantities, they are appropriate for the entire family.

HEARTY DINNERS

Anchovy Prega*
Roger Staubach's Beef Stroganoff**
Brown Rice with Mushrooms*
Deviled Brussels Sprouts*
Oasis Salad*
Milk or Coffee

Romaine Citrus Salad*
Liver Again**
Rice
Oriental Green Beans*
Lemon Dessert*
Iced Tea

Avacado Salad Mold*
Marcia Mecklenberg's Chicken Breasts
   in Orange Sauce**
Broad Noodles
Broiled Tomatoes with Dill Sauce*
Jefferson Davis Pie*
Milk

Recipes from football players:

Jack Youngblood's Fillet of Black Cod,
Italian Style*
   All-pro defensive end for the Los Angeles Rams

Ken Stabler's Oven-Beef Burgundy Stew**
   Quarterback for the Oakland Raiders

Roger Staubach's Beef Stroganoff**
   Quarterback for the Dallas Cowboys

**In this chapter
*See Index

Roger Staubach's Beef Stroganoff

1 lb beef tenderloin (½ kg)
2 Tbsp butter or margarine (30 ml)
½ lb mushrooms (225 g)
1 medium onion, minced
10½-oz condensed beef broth (300 ml)
2 Tbsp catsup (30 ml)
1 small clove garlic, minced
1 tsp salt (5 ml)
3 Tbsp flour (45 ml)
1 c dairy sour cream (240 ml)
¼ c cooking sherry (60 ml)
3 to 4 cups hot cooked noodles (750 ml)

Cut meat across the grain into narrow (½-inch) strips, about 1½-inches long (4 cm). Melt butter in large skillet. Wash and slice mushrooms and saute with onion until onion is tender, then remove from skillet. In same skillet, saute meat until light brown. Remove and add to sauteed vegetables. Reserving ⅓ of the broth, stir in remaining broth, the catsup, garlic and salt. Cover; simmer 15 minutes.

Blend reserved broth and ⅔'s of the flour; stir into pan adding meat, mushrooms and onion. Heat to boiling, stirring constantly. Boil and stir 1 minute. Reduce heat. Add remaining flour to sour cream and when blended, add to pan with sherry. Bring back to the boil. Serve over noodles.

Serves 4.

Calories per serving: approximately 480.

Roger Staubach is quarterback for the champion Dallas Cowboys.

Brisket Barbecue

5 lb beef brisket (2 kg)
2 tsp salt (10 ml)
½ c catsup (120 ml)
¼ c vinegar (60 ml)j
½ c finely chopped onion (120 ml)
1 bay leaf, crumbled
Freshly cracked pepper

Rub meat with salt. Place on double, heavy duty foil. Mix remaining ingredients and rub into meat. Seal foil securely. Grill 5 inches above medium coals. Turn once. Cook 1½ hours or until meat is tender.

Serves 10.

Calories per serving: approximately 320.

Beef a la Grecque

2½ lb lean beef stew meat (1 kg)
2 Tbsp oil (30 ml)
1 tsp salt (5 ml)
1 tsp oregano (5 ml)
½ tsp pepper (3 ml)
1 clove garlic
1 bay leaf
2 strips lemon peel
1 c beef broth (240 ml)
8-oz tomato sauce (240 ml)
1 c water (240 ml)
16-oz canned small whole onions (450 g)
2 Tbsp cornstarch (30 ml)
2 Tbsp water (30 ml)
1 c walnut halves (240 ml)
½ lb Muenster cheese, cut in ½-inch cubes
  (240 g)

Cut beef in cubes (3 × 3 cm). Brown slowly in oil. Add salt, oregano, pepper, garlic, bay leaf, lemon peel, broth, tomato sauce and water; heat to boiling. Cover and simmer until beef is tender, about 2 hours. Drain onions and add to stew. Stir cornstarch into remaining water and stir into stew. Cook 2 or 3 minutes longer; add walnuts and cheese and serve at once.

Serves 6.

Calories per serving: approximately 900.

Fruited Pot Roast

4 to 5 lb pot roast (arm or blade)
2 Tbsp oil (30 ml)
½ c chopped onion (60 - 70 g)
½ c chopped carrot (70 g)
¼ c dry red wine or beef broth (60 ml)
1 clove garlic, minced
Salt and pepper
1 c chopped dried figs (170 g)
½ c dried apricots (75 g)
1 c raisins (150 g)
1½ c water (360 ml)

In heavy skillet, brown meat on both sides in hot oil. Add onion, carrots, wine, garlic and sprinkle with salt and pepper. Place fruit on top of meat, add water, cover with lid or foil and place in 225°F (115°C) oven for 5 hours.

Serves 8 generously.

Calories per serving: approximately 600.

Deanna Coleman's Oven Beef Stew

1 lb stew meat (450 g)
10½-oz frozen mixed vegetables (315 g)
3 potatoes, quartered
1 onion
1 lb carrots (450 g)
2 Tbsp tapioca (30 ml)
3 c tomato juice (720 ml)
Salt and pepper to taste

Put meat and vegetables in a dutch oven. Add tapioca and tomato juice. Mix well. Cover and place in oven at 250 °F (125 °C) for 6 hours. Do not stir.

Serves 4.

Calories per serving: approximately 400.

Deanna Coleman is a record holder for the 800 meter and mile in high school.

Ken Stabler's Oven-Beef Burgundy Stew

2 Tbsp soy sauce (30 ml)
2 Tbsp flour (30 ml)
2 lb beef stew meat (1 kg)
4 carrots
2 large onions
1 sliced stalk celery
1 clove garlic, minced
¼ tsp pepper (1 ml)
¼ tsp thyme (1 ml)
1 c dry red wine (240 ml)
1 c sliced mushrooms (240 ml)

Blend soy sauce with flour in baking dish. Cut meat into small cubes and add to soy sauce mixture. Toss to coat meat. Cut carrots in chunks and add. Slice onions and add with celery, garlic, seasonings, and wine. Stir. Cover and bake at 325 °F (150 °C) for 1 hour. Add mushrooms and bake for 1½ or 2 hours longer or until meat is tender. Great served on rice or noodles.

Serves 6.

Calories per serving: approximately 350.

Ken Stabler is quarterback for the champion Oakland Raiders.

Beef Vegetable Pie

1½ lb beef stew meat (720 g)
3 Tbsp salad oil (45 ml)
2 onions, sliced
3 cloves garlic, minced
1 tsp salt (5 ml)
2 Tbsp sherry (optional) (30 ml)
¼ tsp black pepper (1 ml)
2 Tbsp soy sauce (30 ml)
1 c beef broth (240 ml)
1 c flour (240 ml)
⅓ c lard or hydrogenated shortening (80 ml)
3 Tbsp water (45 ml)
4 carrots, sliced
1 green pepper, chopped
8 cherry tomatoes
6 green onions, cut in 1-inch pices
3 Tbsp cornstarch (45 ml)
3 Tbsp water (45 ml)

Brown beef in oil. Add sliced onions, garlic, salt, sherry, pepper, soy sauce and broth. Cover and simmer until meat is tender, about 2 hours. Prepare pastry by cutting lard into flour and adding enough water to form a dough. Roll out pastry to fit top of pie pan, cover with plastic wrap and chill. Add vegetables to the cooked meat. Combine cornstarch and water, add to vegetables and meat mixture. Bring to boil. Place in 10-inch (29 cm) pie pan and top the mixture with chilled pastry. Cut a vent in top of pastry and bake at 450°F (225°C) for 25 to 35 minutes or until crust is golden brown.

Serves 6.

Calories per serving: approximately 700.

Hunter Stew

4 dried mushrooms
¼ c water (60 ml)
1 lb pork or beef, sliced (450 g)
1 Tbsp oil (15 ml)
1 lb sauerkraut, drained (450 g)
1 tsp beef soup base mix (5 ml)
1 link Polish sausage
1 lb fresh cabbage, shredded (450 g)
¼ lb bacon, diced (120 g)
1 lg onion, sliced
2 Tbsp flour (30 ml)
2 Tbsp water (30 ml)
3 Tbsp tomato paste (45 ml)
Salt and pepper to taste
½ c red wine (120 ml)

Place mushrooms in small bowl; pour boiling water over them and allow to stand for 30 minutes. Chop fine and set aside. Brown meat in oil. Add the sauerkraut, beef soup base, sausage and mushrooms. Cook cabbage in a small amount of water until it is tender. Drain and add to sauerkraut mixture. Fry bacon and onion until brown. Add the flour and water, tomato paste and salt and pepper, adding more water if necessary. Add to the sauerkraut. Add wine and simmer an additional 10 minutes. Serve with potatoes and rye bread.

Serves 6.

Calories per serving: approximately 450.

Pork Satay

8 Brazil nuts
⅛ tsp red pepper (1 ml)
2 Tbsp ground coriander (30 ml)
¼ tsp black pepper (2 ml)
1 clove garlic
2 Tbsp chopped onion (30 ml)
1 tsp salt (5 ml)
1 Tbsp brown sugar (15 ml)
3 Tbsp lemon juice (45 ml)
¼ c soy sauce (60 ml)
1½ lb pork (750 g)

Grind Brazil nuts very fine. Mix with remaining ingredients except the pork. Cut pork into 1½-inch (4 cm) cubes and add to marinade. Mix well and let stand 2 - 3 hours. String on skewers and broil slowly 20 - 25 minutes until done.

Serves 5 - 6.

Calories per serving: approximately 500.

Peanut Packed Pork Chops

1 c croutons (240 ml)
½ c salted peanuts, finely chopped (120 ml)
2 Tbsp minced onion (30 ml)
2 Tbsp snipped parsley (30 ml)
1 tsp crushed red chili pepper (5 ml)
⅓ c butter or margarine, melted (80 ml)
1 Tbsp water (15 ml)
½ tsp salt (3 ml)
8 loin or rib pork chops, 1¼-inch (3 cm) thick,
   with pockets
1 tsp salt (3 ml)
Pepper, freshly ground
10-oz apple jelly (275 g)
2 Tbsp lemon juice (30 ml)

Mix croutons, peanuts, onion, parsley and chili pepper in bowl. Stir butter, water and salt together; pour over crouton mixture and toss. Trim fat from chops, rub in salt and pepper. Stuff crouton mixture in pockets, closing with toothpicks or skewers. Heat jelly and lemon juice to boiling. Place chops on barbeque grill over medium coals. Cook one hour, turning every 15 minutes. Baste with jelly sauce during the last 30 minutes of cooking. Chops may also be baked in the oven at 350 °F (175 °C) for one hour or until done.

Serves 8.

Calories per serving: approximately 540.

Pork Kabobs

½ c chutney (120 ml)
¼ c catsup (60 ml)
1 Tbsp soy sauce (15 ml)
4 drops Tabasco
2 Tbsp salad oil (30 ml)
2 lb boneless pork loin (1 kg)
12 small mushrooms
1 green pepper, cut in 1-inch (2.5 cm) squares

Blend chutney, catsup, soy sauce, Tabasco and oil in blender. Blend until smooth. Pour into bowl. Cut meat into 1-inch (2.5 cm) cubes. Add meat to marinade and let stand several hours, turning occasionally. Put meat, mushrooms and green pepper on 6 skewers. Barbecue over medium coals 15 - 20 minutes. Serve with steamed rice.

Serves 6.

Calories per serving: approximately 350.

Portuguese Spareribs in Garlic Wine

4 lbs country-style spareribs (2 kg)
1 c cider vinegar (240 ml)
2 c water (480 ml)
½ c dry white wine (120 ml)
2 tsp crushed whole coriander (10 ml)
2 tsp crushed whole cumin (10 ml)
5 - 6 cloves garlic
¼ tsp cayenne (1 ml)
2 tsp salt (10 ml)

Put spareribs in a deep non-metal bowl. Blend together vinegar, water, wine, coriander, cumin, garlic cloves (slightly broken), cayenne, and salt. Pour liquid over pork. Cover and refrigerate for 3 hours; turn meat several times during this period. Remove meat from marinade and let drain for about 30 minutes. Discard all liquid. Arrange meat in a single layer in a roasting pan and broil over medium heat until done.

Serves 4.

Calories per serving: approximately 400.

Stuffed Spareribs

3½ lb spareribs (1½ kg)
1 Tbsp salt (15 ml)
Freshly ground black pepper
1 lb pitted dried prunes, halved (450 g)
4 apples, peeled, cored and cut into ½-inch (1.2 cm) thick slices
½ tsp basil (3 ml)
2 c bread cubes (480 ml)
¼ c light-brown sugar (60 ml)
1 tsp ground cinnamon (5 ml)

Preheat the oven to 350°F (175°C). Sprinkle the meaty sides of the spareribs with ⅔'s of the salt and a few grindings of pepper. Place 1 strip of ribs meat side down. Mix together prunes, apples, bread and basil and spread evenly over meat. Sprinkle with the brown sugar, the remaining salt, and the cinnamon. Cover with the other strip of spareribs, meat side up. Tie the 2 together, crosswise and lengthwise, securely enclosing the stuffing. Place the ribs on a rack set in a shallow roasting pan and bake in the middle of the oven for 1 hour or until done. Cut away the strings and serve the spareribs.

Serves 4.

Calories per serving: approximately 750.

Savory Short Ribs with Cornmeal Dumplings

3 lb beef short ribs, or pork ribs (1½ kg)
Salt and pepper to taste
1 medium onion, cut in wedges
1 clove garlic, minced
28-oz can red tomatoes, diced (840 g)
12-oz can of beer (360 ml)
1 green chili pepper, finely chopped
1 Tbsp soy sauce (30 ml)
1 Tbsp sugar (15 ml)
½ tsp salt (3 ml)
¼ tsp pepper (1 ml)
¼ tsp nutmeg (1 ml)

Dumplings

1 c water (240 ml)
½ c yellow cornmeal (120 ml)
½ tsp salt (3 ml)
1 egg, beaten
½ c all-purpose flour (120 ml)
1 tsp baking powder (5 ml)
Dash of pepper
7-oz can whole-kernel corn, drained (210 g)

Cut ribs into serving-size pieces. Brown and season with salt and pepper. Remove ribs and discard fat, reserving 2 tablespoons. Add onion and garlic and saute. Add tomatoes, beer, chili pepper, soy sauce, sugar, salt, pepper and nutmeg. Return meat to pan and simmer for 2 hours. In saucepan, combine water, cornmeal and salt and bring to a boil. Cook and stir until thickened. Remove from heat and stir ¼ c (60 ml) of hot mixture into beaten egg. Return to mixture. Stir together the flour, baking powder and a dash of pepper. Add to cornmeal mixture and beat well. Stir in corn. Drop batter by table-spoonfuls onto boiling stew mixture. Cover and simmer for 12 minutes, or until dumplings are done.

Serves 6 - 8.

Calories per serving: approximately 415.

Company Strata

12 slices toasted whole wheat bread
12 oz sharp process cheese, sliced (350 g)
10-oz pkg frozen chopped broccoli, cooked
   and drained (300 g)
2 c diced cooked ham (480 ml)
6 eggs, slightly beaten
3½ c milk (850 ml)
2 Tbsp onion, minced (30 ml)
½ tsp salt (3 ml)
¼ tsp dry mustard (2 ml)

Cut toast into squares. Place ⅓ in the bottom of a 13 × 9-inch (32 × 23 cm) baking dish. Layer cheese, broccoli, ham and remaining bread. Combine eggs, milk, onion, salt and mustard and pour over bread. Bake at 325°F (165°C) for 55 minutes. Let stand 10 minutes before cutting.

Serves 12.

Calories per serving: approximately 255.

Swiss Turkey Bake

½ c chopped onion (120 ml)
2 Tbsp butter (30 ml)
3 Tbsp all-purpose flour (45 ml)
½ tsp salt (3 ml)
¼ tsp pepper (1 ml)
½ c canned sliced mushrooms, undrained
   (120 ml)
1 c milk (240 ml)
2 Tbsp dry sherry (30 ml)
3 c cubed cooked turkey (720 ml)
5 oz water chestnuts, sliced (150 g)
2 oz Swiss cheese, shredded (60 g)
1½ c soft bread crumbs (360 ml)
3 Tbsp butter (45 ml)

In a skillet, cook onion in 2 Tbsp (30 ml) butter; blend in flour, salt, pepper, mushrooms, milk and sherry and cook until thickened. Add turkey and water chestnuts. Pour into 1½ qt (1½ liter) casserole, top with cheese, bread crumbs and dot with butter. Bake at 400°F (200°C) for 25 minutes.

Serves 6.

Calories per serving: approximately 345.

Marcia Mecklenberg's Chicken Breasts in Orange Sauce

6 chicken breasts
¼ c all-purpose flour (60 ml)
¼ tsp paprika (1 ml)
¼ tsp garlic powder (1 ml)
½ tsp salt (3 ml)
⅓ c oil (80 ml)
¼ lb fresh mushrooms (120 g)
10½-oz condensed cream of chicken soup
  (300 g)
½ c chicken broth (120 ml)
½ c orange juice (120 ml)
1 c dry white wine (120 ml)
1 Tbsp brown sugar (15 ml)
2 c sliced carrots (480 ml)

Roll chicken breasts in flour and sprinkle with paprika, garlic powder and salt. Heat oil and brown chicken on both sides. Remove excess oil and add remaining ingredients. Cover and simmer about 40 minutes or until chicken is tender.

Serves 6.

Calories per serving: approximately 340.

Marcia Mecklenberg is the U.S. Indoor 2nd place contender in shot, 4th ranked in the U.S.

Baked Chicken with Yogurt Sauce

4 whole chicken breasts
2 Tbsp oil (30 ml)
½ c chopped onions (120 ml)
1 clove minced garlic
½ lb sliced fresh mushrooms (225 g)
1 tsp salt (5 ml)
½ tsp pepper (3 ml)
2 c yogurt (480 ml)

Brown chicken in oil over medium heat (about 3 - 5 minutes); remove to shallow baking pan. Saute onions, garlic and mushrooms in remaining oil. Lower heat. Add salt, pepper and yogurt. Stir to blend. Pour over chicken. Bake at 350 °F (175 °C) for 40 minutes or until chicken is done.

Serves 4.

Calories per serving: approximately 340.

Goal-to-Go Fried Chicken

1½ c poultry stuffing mix (360 ml)
2 Tbsp Parmesan cheese (30 ml)
¼ c butter or margarine, melted (60 ml)
1 garlic clove, crushed
6 - 8 chicken pieces

Crush stuffing mix in blender or with rolling pin. Stir in cheese. Melt butter with garlic. Dip chicken in butter, then in crumbs. Bake uncovered at 350 °F (175 °C) for 1 hour.

Serves 4.

Calories per serving: approximately 350.

Cornish Game Hens and Rice

1 c long-grain rice (240 ml)
1 envelope Italian salad dressing mix
2½ c boiling water (600 ml)
10½-oz can cream of chicken soup (290 g)
2 cornish game hens
4 pineapple spears (optional)

Spread rice in a 3-quart (3 liter) shallow baking dish and bake at 375 °F (185 °C) for 15 minutes, stirring occasionally, until golden. Combine salad dressing mix with boiling water and the chicken soup, then stir into rice. Cut game hens in half, lengthwise. Season to taste with salt and pepper. Place game hens, cut side down, on top of rice. Cover dish tightly with foil. Bake at 350 °F (175 °C) for 30 minutes. Uncover, bake for 30 minutes longer or until rice and hens are tender. Serve with pineapple spears and fresh broccoli, if desired.

Serves 4.

Calories per serving: approximately 440.

Curry-lovers Chicken

⅓ c frozen orange juice concentrate (80 ml)
1 tsp salt (5 ml)
1 egg, slightly beaten
6 pieces of chicken
1 c bran flake cereal (unsweetened) (240 ml)
½ c shredded coconut (120 ml)
1 tsp curry (5 ml)
¼ c butter, melted (60 ml)
Orange slices

Mix together orange juice concentrate, salt and egg. Add chicken and marinate 15 minutes. Remove chicken and reserve marinade. Mix bran cereal, coconut and curry and coat chicken with mixture, patting in well. Place on lightly oiled, foil lined pan and drizzle with butter and marinade. Cover pan and bake at 350 °F (175 °C) for 30 minutes. Uncover and bake 30 to 40 minutes longer or until well browned. Garnish with orange slices.

Serves 6.

Calories per serving: approximately 300.

Dave Cowens' Baked Chicken Breasts

4 oz chipped beef (120 ml)
8 chicken breasts, boned
8 strips bacon
½ pt sour cream (240 ml)
10½-oz cream of mushroom soup (280 g)
¼ c white wine (60 ml)

Line bottom of buttered 9 × 13-inch (23 × 32 cm) baking dish with chipped beef. Top with chicken breasts. Cover chicken breasts with bacon. Make a sauce with remaining ingredients and pour over chicken breasts. Bake for 1 hour at 375 °F (185 °C).

Serves 8.

Calories per serving: approximately 400.

Dave Cowens plays center for the Boston Celtics.

Lamb Breast with Artichokes

6 lb lamb breast (2.5 kg)
2 onions, finely chopped
¼ lb butter (120 g)
1 tsp dill weed (6 ml)
2 lemons
Salt and pepper
5 c water (1¼ liter)
3 egg yolks
1 tsp cornstarch (5 ml)
12 artichoke hearts, frozen or canned

Saute lamb and onion in half the butter. Add dill weed and 1 sliced lemon, salt and pepper to taste. Add water, cover and simmer for 1½ hours. Drain off liquid and reserve 3 cups. Discard cooked lemon pieces. Add artichoke hearts and remaining butter to the cooked meat and simmer for 30 minutes. Mix egg yolks, juice of the other lemon, cornstarch. Slowly add 3 cups cooled broth, mixing well. Cook over low heat, stirring constantly until thickened. Pour sauce over lamb and artichokes.

Serves 8.

Calories per serving: approximately 475.

Sweet-Sour Chicken

2 tsp cornstarch (10 ml)
⅔ c cold water (160 ml)
½ c sugar (120 ml)
½ tsp soy sauce (3 ml)
Dash garlic salt
⅛ tsp ground ginger (1 ml)
⅛ tsp pepper (1 ml)
3 Tbsp catsup (45 ml)
2 Tbsp vinegar (30 ml)
2 c cooked chicken, 1-inch (2.5 cm) cubes
1 c pineapple chunks (240 ml)
½ green pepper, sliced
1 tomato, chopped
1 Tbsp sesame seeds (15 ml)
1½ c cooked rice (360 ml)

Combine cornstarch and water; mix thoroughly. Add sugar, soy sauce, garlic salt, ginger, pepper, catsup and vinegar. Stir to blend. Cook over medium heat, stirring constantly, until sauce thickens. Add chicken, pineapple, green pepper and tomato to sauce and simmer until ingredients are warmed through. Stir gently once or twice to prevent sticking. Pour into shallow serving dish. Garnish with sesame seeds. Serve with rice.

Serves 6 - 8.

Calories per serving: approximately 300.

Meat Loaf

1½ lb lean ground beef (700 g)
8-oz tomato sauce (225 g)
1 egg
1½ tsp salt (7 ml)
1½ tsp Worcestershire sauce (7 ml)
1 c oatmeal (240 ml)
1 medium onion, finely chopped
¼ tsp pepper (1 ml)
¼ tsp oregano (1 ml)
½ tsp garlic salt (3 ml)

Mix ingredients together lightly. Place in 9 × 5-inch (23 × 12 cm) loaf pan and bake for 1 hour 15 minutes at 350°F (175°C). May be served warm or cold. For variety, try one of the meat loaf fillings.

Serves 4 - 6.

Calories per serving: approximately 250.

Italian Style

¼ c chopped green peppers (60 ml)
12-oz cottage cheese (340 g)
8 oz Mozzarella cheese (225 g)
10 ripe, pitted olives

Mix green peppers, cottage cheese, Mozzarella cheese and olives together well. With a spoon scoop out a layer of meat from the center of the meat loaf. Spoon in all of the filling; cover with remaining meat. Bake in loaf pan at 350°F (175°C) for 1 hour and 15 minutes. Let stand at least 10 minutes before slicing.

Calories per serving: approximately 450.

Mushroom Style

½ lb fresh mushrooms (225 g)
2 stalks celery
1 medium onion
2 Tbsp butter or margarine (30 ml)
½ c catsup or tomato juice (120 ml)
1½ slices bread
½ tsp salt (3 ml)
⅛ tsp pepper

Chop mushrooms, celery and onion and saute in butter until vegetables are limp. Add catsup or tomato juice and simmer 10 minutes. Break bread into small pieces. Add bread, salt and pepper to vegetable mixture. Scoop out center of meat loaf and spoon in filling. Cover with remaining meat. Bake at 350°F (175°C) for 1 hour and 15 minutes. Serve topped with additional tomato sauce, if desired.

Calories per serving: approximately 375.

Globetrotter Lasagne

1 onion, chopped
3 Tbsp olive oil (45 ml)
1 lb lean ground beef (450 g)
½ lb pork sausage (225 g)
1 clove garlic, minced
8-oz can tomato sauce (225 g)
3½-oz can tomato paste (100 g)
1 c dry red wine (240 ml)
1 tsp salt (5 ml)
2 bay leaves
½ tsp oregano (3 ml)
½ tsp freshly ground pepper (3 ml)
½ tsp sugar (3 ml)
½ tsp thyme (3 ml)
½ tsp basil (3 ml)
12 oz lasagne noodles (360 g)
2 c ricotta cheese (480 ml)
10-oz pkg spinach, drained (optional) (300 g)
½ lb Mozzarella cheese (225 g)
6 large mushrooms, thinly sliced, sauteed in oil
½ c Parmesan cheese (120 ml)

Saute onion in oil until transparent; add beef, sausage and garlic and stir until meat is brown and crumbly. Add tomato sauce, tomato paste, wine, salt and bay leaves. Simmer for two hours.

Add oregano, pepper, sugar, thyme and basil and continue cooking for 30 minutes. Cool and remove bay leaves. Cook noodles according to package directions. Drain and rinse with cold water. Arrange ⅓ of the noodles in the bottom of a 9 × 13-inch (23 × 32 cm) pan. Spread ⅓ of the tomato sausage sauce over the noodles, top with ½ of the ricotta cheese, spinach and Mozzarella cheese. Repeat layering and top with mushrooms and Parmesan cheese. Bake uncovered, 350 °F (175 °C) for 30 minutes.

Calories per serving: approximately 530.

A favorite of Hubert "Geese" Ausbie, all-time player for the Globetrotters.

Mock Lasagne

1 lb hamburger (450 g)
1 onion, chopped
2 cloves garlic, minced
2 c tomato sauce (480 ml)
1 tsp salt (5 ml)
2 tsp sugar (10 ml)
¼ tsp pepper (1 ml)
½ tsp basil (2 ml)
1 c cream-style cottage cheese (240 ml)
1 8-oz pkg cream cheese (225 g)
¼ c sour cream (60 ml)
½ tsp oregano (3 ml)
½ c sliced green onions (120 ml)
½ c chopped green pepper (120 ml)
10 or 12-oz pkg wide egg noodles (300 g)
½ c grated Parmesan cheese (120 ml)

Saute hamburger, onion and garlic until meat is brown. Remove excess fat. Add tomato sauce, salt, sugar, pepper and basil and simmer for 15 minutes. Set aside. In a bowl, combine cottage cheese, cream cheese, sour cream, oregano, green onions and green pepper. Cook noodles according to package directions; rinse in cold water and drain. Place half the cooked noodles in a greased 2 quart (2 liter) baking dish. Spread on one cup of the meat mixture. Cover with cheese mixture. Place remaining noodles on top and then the rest of the meat sauce. Sprinkle with the Parmesan cheese. Bake at 350 °F (175 °C) for about 40 minutes.

Serves 8.

Calories per serving: approximately 425.

Shipwreck Casserole

2 medium potatoes, sliced
2 small onions, sliced
½ c celery, chopped (120 g)
¼ c rice, uncooked (60 ml)
1 lb raw hamburger (450 g)
1 lb can red kidney beans, undrained (450 g)
2 c tomato juice (480 ml)
Salt
Pepper

In greased casserole put ingredients in layers in the following order: potatoes, onions, celery, rice, hamburger, kidney beans and tomato juice. Salt and pepper may be added between layers. Cover and bake at 350 °F (175 °C) for 1½ hours.

Serves 4.

Calories per serving: approximately 500.

Deep Dish Pizza

Yeast dough for 1 loaf bread
2 Tbsp cornmeal (optional) (30 ml)
1¼-oz pkg spaghetti sauce mix (35 g)
6-oz can tomato paste (180 g)
2 c water (480 ml)
1-2 Tbsp oil (30 ml)
2 lb Italian sausage (1 kg)
2 lb Mozarella cheese (1 kg)
2 c sliced fresh mushrooms (480 ml)
2 onions, sliced
2 green peppers, sliced
2 tsp oregano (10 ml)

Divide dough in half. Roll out each half in 13-inch (32 cm) circle and place on lightly greased (sprinkle with cornmeal if desired) pizza pans or cookie sheets. Prepare spaghetti sauce with tomato paste, water and oil, and set aside to cool. Brown Italian sausage and remove excess fat. Spread sauce on circles. Place half of the Mozarella cheese on top of each of the pieces of dough. Top with cooked sausage, mushrooms, onions and green peppers. Add remaining cheese and sprinkle with oregano. Bake at 400°F (200°C) for 25 minutes.

Makes 2 pizzas.

Calories per pizza: approximately 1500.

Stuffed Manicotti

1 lb lean ground beef
½ c chopped onion (120 ml)
1 large clove garlic, minced
12 oz tomato paste (360 g)
2 c water (480 ml)
2 Tbsp chopped parsley (30 ml)
1 Tbsp basil (15 ml)
½ tsp salt (3 ml)
Dash of freshly ground pepper
1 c cream-style cottage cheese (240 ml)
⅔ c grated Monterey Jack cheese (180 ml)
2 eggs, slightly beaten
¼ c chopped parsley (60 ml)
½ tsp salt (3 ml)
½ tsp pepper (3 ml)
14 manicotti shells
½ c grated Parmesan cheese (60 ml)

Brown meat lightly in large saucepan, draining off excess fat. Add onion, garlic, tomato paste, water, parsley, basil, salt and pepper. Cook shells until just tender; drain and rinse. Stuff manicotti with cheese mixture. Pour half the meat sauce into a 9 × 13-inch (23 × 33 cm) baking pan. Arrange stuffed manicotti in a row. Top with remaining sauce and sprinkle with Parmesan cheese. Bake at 350°F (175°C) for 35 minutes.

Serves 8.

Calories per serving: approximately 410.

Teresa Smith's Mexican Sunday Night Supper

2 Tbsp salad oil (30 ml)
1½ lb lean ground beef (750 g)
1 small onion, diced
1 can (10-oz) mild enchilada sauce (280 g)
4-oz black olives, sliced (100 g)
8-oz corn (225 g)
2 fresh tomatoes, thinly sliced
1 Tbsp green chilies, chopped (15 ml)
¼ tsp oregano (1 ml)
¼ tsp cumin (1 ml)
¼ tsp garlic powder (1 ml)
¼ tsp chili powder (1 ml)
1 c grated Monterey Jack cheese (240 ml)
1 c grated Cheddar cheese (240 ml)
6 large corn tortillas

Heat oil in large skillet, add ground beef and cook until beef loses red color. Add onion, enchilada sauce, olives, corn, tomatoes and chilies. Add oregano, cumin, garlic powder and chili powder. Simmer for 5 minutes. Line a 9 × 9-inch (23 × 23 cm) pan with 3 tortillas, pour half of meat sauce over tortillas and sprinkle with half of the two cheeses. Repeat layers. Bake at 325 °F (165 °C) for 30 minutes.

Serves 8.

Calories per serving: approximately 430.

Teresa Smith is U.S. Women's Pentathlete record holder.

10th Inning Casserole

1 lb ground beef (450 g)
10-oz frozen peas, thawed (280 g)
2 c finely sliced raw celery (480 ml)
1 small onion, finely chopped
10½-oz condensed mushroom soup (315 g)
2 Tbsp milk (30 ml)
¾ tsp salt (4 ml)
¼ tsp pepper (1 ml)
½ c unsweetened granola (120 ml)

Cook ground beef in pan until brown. Place in 1½-qt (1½ liter) casserole. Place peas, celery and onion on top of meat. Mix together mushroom soup, milk, salt, pepper and pour over vegetables. Top with granola. Bake at 375 °F (185 °C) for 30 minutes.

Serves 6.

Calories per serving: approximately 240.

Spinach Meatballs

Meatballs:

1½ lbs lean ground beef (750 g)
⅔ c chopped onion (160 ml)
1 garlic bud, minced
10-oz pkg frozen spinach (300 g), squeezed
   dry
½ c bread crumbs (120 ml)
¼ c Parmesan cheese, grated (60 ml)
1 egg
1 tsp salt (5 ml)
1 tsp freshly ground pepper (3 ml)
½ tsp MSG (3 ml)
3 Tbsp oil (45 ml)

Combine beef, onion, garlic, spinach, bread crumbs, cheese, egg, and seasonings. Shape into balls using approximately 2 Tbsp (30 ml) for each. Fry in oil. Brown well. Cover with tomato sauce.

Tomato Sauce:

3 Tbsp flour (45 ml)
6-oz tomato paste (180 g)
1½ c water (360 ml)
¼ tsp MSG (2 ml)
½ tsp salt (3 ml)
½ tsp oregano (3 ml)
3 Tbsp parsley (45 ml)

Combine ingredients and cook, stirring constantly until bubbly. Add sauce to browned meat balls. Cook for about 5 minutes.

Serves 6.

Calories per serving: approximately 400.

Barbecued Beef Balls

1½ lbs lean ground beef (750 g)
¾ c rolled oats (180 ml)
1 c milk (240 ml)
1 Tbsp minced onion (15 ml)
1½ tsp salt (7 ml)
⅛ tsp pepper (1 ml)
½ c all-purpose flour (120 ml)
3 Tbsp oil (45 ml)
2 Tbsp sugar (30 ml)
2 Tbsp Worcestershire sauce (30 ml)
1 c tomato sauce (240 ml)
½ c water (120 ml)
¼ c vinegar (60 ml)
½ c minced onion (120 ml)

Combine meat, oats, milk, onion, salt and pepper. Shape into balls. Roll in flour and brown in oil. Arrange in oiled 2 quart (2 liter) baking dish. Combine remaining ingredients. Pour over meat balls. Bake at 350 °F (175 °C) for about 35 minutes.

Serves 6 - 8.

Calories per serving: approximately 400.

Pre-game Fish Bake

1 lb fish fillets (450 g)
Salt and pepper
½ c flour (120 ml)
½ c cornmeal (120 ml)
¼ c wheat germ (60 ml)
1 tsp salt (5 ml)
½ tsp pepper (3 ml)
1 egg, beaten
2 Tbsp butter (15 ml)

Cut fish into 4 portions. Sprinkle lightly with salt and pepper. Combine flour, cornmeal, wheat germ, salt and pepper. Dip each portion lightly in egg and seasoned mixture, and repeat again. Place coated fish in lightly buttered baking dish. Dot with butter and bake at 425 °F (212 °C) about 15-20 minutes or until fish is done.

Serves 4.

Calories per serving: approximately 350.

Mexican Seafood Gumbo

¼ lb bacon (120 g)
¼ c chopped onion (60 ml)
¼ c diced green pepper (60 ml)
1 c diced celery (240 ml)
4 tomatoes, diced
4 c chicken broth (1 liter)
6½-oz canned shrimp, drained (190 g)
7-oz canned Dungeness crab (210 g)
15-oz canned okra (430 g)
1 c cooked rice (240 ml)
Salt and pepper

Dice and saute bacon in large soup pot with onion, green pepper and celery. Add tomatoes, broth, shrimp, crab, okra and rice. Simmer for 20 minutes. Season to taste and serve.

Serves 6.

Calories per serving: approximately 175.

Seafood Quiche

Whole wheat pastry*
4 oz Swiss cheese, shredded (120 g)
4 oz Gruyere cheese, shredded (120 g)
1 Tbsp all-purpose flour (15 ml)
3 eggs
1 c light cream (240 ml)
½ tsp prepared mustard (2 ml)
¼ tsp Worcestershire sauce (1 ml)
1 dash hot pepper sauce (bottled)
½ tsp salt (2 ml)
Dash of pepper
7-oz can tiny shrimp (210 g)
6-oz can flaked crab meat (180 g)
Parsley

Prepare whole wheat pastry and place in 9-inch (23 cm) pie pan. Toss cheese with flour. Mix eggs, cream, mustard, Worcestershire sauce, hot pepper sauce, salt and pepper. Place ¾ of cheese mixture in pie shell; add seafood and remaining cheese. Pour in egg mixture and bake at 400 °F (200 °C) for 30 minutes or until knife comes out clean. Garnish with parsley.

Serves 6.

Calories per serving: approximately 475.

*See index.

Seattle Salmon Souffle

3 Tbsp butter (45 ml)
3 Tbsp flour (45 ml)
½ tsp curry (2 ml)
Salt and pepper
1 c milk (240 ml)
4 eggs, separated
7-oz canned salmon (200 g)

Melt butter in saucepan; add flour, curry, salt and pepper and cook until bubbly. Add milk and bring to a boil. Remove from surface unit and cool. Beat egg yolks until lemon colored and add to cooled milk mixture. Stir in flaked salmon. Beat egg whites until stiff and fold into mixture; pour into 2½-qt (3 liter) buttered casserole and place in water bath. Bake at 375°F (185°C) for 45 minutes. Serve with creamed peas.

Creamed Peas

1 Tbsp butter (15 ml)
1 Tbsp flour (15 ml)
1 c half and half (240 ml)
Salt to taste
½ tsp curry (2 ml)
10½-oz pkg frozen peas (300 g)

Melt butter in a saucepan; add flour and stir. Add milk and cook until thickened. Add salt, curry and peas and cook until heated through. Spoon over souffle.

Serves 6.

Calories per serving: approximately 220.

Sportsman's Tuna Casserole

20 oz frozen broccoli (570 g)
20 oz canned chunk white albacore tuna,
    drained (570 g)
21 oz canned cream of chicken soup (600 g)
1 c mayonnaise (240 ml)
½ tsp curry powder (3 ml)
1 Tbsp lemon juice (15 ml)
½ c shredded Cheddar cheese (120 ml)
½ c bread crumbs (120 ml)
1 Tbsp melted butter (15 ml)
½ c sliced almonds (120 ml)

Steam broccoli until tender and arrange in buttered 9 × 12 inch (22 × 29 cm) baking dish. Add tuna. Combine soup, mayonnaise, curry, lemon juice and cheese and pour over tuna. Combine bread crumbs and butter with almonds and sprinkle on top. Bake at 350°F (175°C) for 30 minutes.

Serves 8.

Calories per serving: approximately 540.

Peterson Boys' Tuna Casserole

½ c chopped onion (120 ml)
1 Tbsp butter (15 ml)
10½-oz can mushroom soup (300 g)
10-oz evaporated milk (280 ml)
½ c grated Parmesan cheese (120 ml)
1 c sliced fresh mushrooms (240 ml)
7-oz can light chunk tuna (210 g)
¼ c sliced black olives (60 ml)
2 Tbsp chopped parsley (30 ml)
½ tsp salt (3 ml)
¼ tsp pepper (1 ml)
2 c cooked noodles (480 ml)
½ c grated Cheddar cheese (120 ml)

Saute onion in butter until soft. Add soup, milk, cheese, and mushrooms and simmer for 5 minutes. Add remaining ingredients except Cheddar cheese and mix gently, only until blended. Place in greased 2 quart (2 liter) casserole and top with cheese. Bake at 350°F (175°C) for 30 minutes. Garnish with cherry tomatoes and additional parsley, if desired.

Serves 4.

Calories per serving: approximately 460.

Deviled Eggs and Ham

6 hard-cooked eggs
¼ c mayonnaise (60 ml)
1 tsp prepared mustard (5 ml)
¼ tsp salt (1 ml)
Pepper
¼ c butter (60 ml)
¼ c all-purpose flour (60 ml)
2 c milk (480 ml)
1 c Cheddar cheese, shredded (240 ml)
1 c cooked ham, diced (240 ml)
1 c frozen peas (240 ml)
½ c bread crumbs (120 ml)
2 Tbsp butter (30 ml)

Carefully halve eggs, remove yolks and mash with mayonnaise, mustard, salt and pepper. Refill whites. Arrange eggs in ungreased 9 × 9-inch (23 × 23 cm) baking dish. In saucepan, melt butter, blend in flour and gradually stir in milk. Cook until thickened; stir in cheese, ham and peas and pour over eggs. Combine crumbs and butter and top casserole. Bake at 375°F (185°C) for 30 minutes.

Serves 6.

Calories per serving: approximately 480.

Orange Curried Eggs

2 Tbsp minced onion (30 ml)
3 Tbsp butter (45 ml)
3 Tbsp flour (45 ml)
1 tsp curry powder (5 ml)
2 c milk (480 ml)
1 tsp salt (5 ml)
¼ tsp pepper (1 ml)
2 tsp grated orange rind (10 ml)
¼ c orange juice (60 ml)
6 hard-cooked eggs, quartered
3 c hot, fluffy rice (720 ml)
Parsley
½ c cooked bacon (optional) (120 ml)
½ c chopped peanuts (optional) (120 ml)
½ c coconut (optional) (120 ml)
½ c chutney (optional) (120 ml)

Saute onion in butter until tender. Stir in flour, curry and milk. Add salt, pepper, orange rind, juice, and eggs. Heat, stirring gently. Spoon over hot rice, garnishing with parsley. Serve with choice of chopped bacon, peanuts, flaked coconut, or chutney.

Serves 6.

Calories per serving: approximately 330.

Hush-Apple Pups

1 lb link sausages (450 g)
2 c applesauce (480 ml)
1 recipe corn bread (for 8 inch or 20 cm pan)
¼ c Parmesan cheese (60 ml)
1 c maple syrup (240 ml)

Fry sausages in a skillet, pour off fat. Place in 9 inch (22 cm) baking dish. Pour applesauce over sausage. Prepare corn bread and spoon over sausages and applesauce. Sprinkle Parmesan cheese on top. Bake at 350 °F (175 °C) 25 minutes or until done. Cut into pieces and serve with hot maple syrup.

Serves 4.

Calories per serving: approximately 550.

Liver Again

6 slices bacon
1½ lb calves liver (700 g)
½ c flour (120 ml)
1 lg onion, sliced
1 green pepper, seeded and sliced
1 envelope dry onion soup mix
16-oz stewed tomatoes (450 g)
Salt and pepper to taste

Fry bacon until crisp. Remove from pan. Dredge liver in flour and fry 2 minutes each side in bacon drippings. Arrange in 9 × 13-inch (23 × 32 cm) dish. Add onion and green pepper to frying pan and cook until vegetables are limp. Spoon over liver and sprinkle with onion soup mix. Pour tomatoes on top of vegetables and bake at 350 °F (175 °C) for 25 minutes. Add bacon slices just before serving.

Serves 6.

Calories per serving: approximately 250.

Soccer is a fast, tough, exciting game. It requires great physical endurance and high caloric intake for energy! Bread is one of the best long-lasting energy foods...and it can help make almost any meal portable! Bread can be filled or topped and it doesn't require refrigeration, so it's a terrific takealong food.

Once the soccer game begins, it rarely stops. The only player who isn't moving up and down the field with the momentum of the ball is the goalie. Field size and the length of the game vary, depending on the league. Even so, 12 calories per minute of play is a conservative estimate of caloric needs for the soccer player. A pre-event meal four hours before the game will support this intense activity for adults. Children, however need additional nutritional support, and should eat oranges and/or juices at halftime. All players should drink fluids throughout the game. Warm weather play requires greater emphasis on fluid intake...during cold weather, extra calories are needed to maintain body temperature.

The following recipes are imaginative sandwich meals to perk up soccer players large and small, before that important game!

Portable Bread with Fillings

Phoenix Sunflower Seed Bread**
A Really Good Marmalade
       or
Peanut Butter Sandwich Fillings*

Recipe from a soccer player:

Kyle Rote's Texas Tacos*
   Soccer player for the Dallas Tornadoes,
   A.B.C. Super Star

50% Whole Wheat Bread**
A Thin Slice of Cheese
Lettuce Leaves
Cooked Turkey
Jellied Cranberry Sauce

Apple-Orange Bread**
Drained Crushed Pineapple
Cream Cheese

**In this chapter
*See Index

Herb and Cheese Bread

½ c milk (120 ml)
2 Tbsp sugar (30 ml)
1 tsp salt (5 ml)
1 Tbsp butter (15 ml)
1 pkg active dry yeast
½ c warm water (120 ml)
1 c all-purpose flour (240 ml)
1 c whole wheat flour (240 ml)
1 tsp dill weed (5 ml)
½ tsp rosemary (3 ml)
½ c grated Cheddar cheese (120 ml)

Scald milk; pour over sugar, salt and butter and cool. Soften yeast in warm water, add to cooled milk mixture. Stir together the all-purpose flour, whole wheat flour, dill weed, rosemary and cheese. Combine all mixtures. Beat vigorously for 5 minutes. Cover with cloth and raise for 1 hour. Transfer to a well-greased 9 × 5-inch (23 × 13 cm) pan and let raise for 10 minutes. Bake at 350 °F (175 °C) for about 1 hour or until done.

Makes 1 loaf.

Calories per serving: approximately 75.

50% Whole Wheat Bread

1 pkg active dry yeast
¼ c lukewarm water (60 ml)
¼ c sugar (60 ml)
2 tsp salt (10 ml)
2 Tbsp shortening (30 ml)
1 c milk (240 ml)
1 c boiling water (240 ml)
2½ c unsifted all-purpose flour (600 ml)
3 c unsifted whole wheat flour (720 ml)

Dissolve yeast in lukewarm water. In another bowl, mix sugar, salt, shortening, milk and boiling water. Let cool. When milk mixture is lukewarm, add yeast and the all-purpose flour. Slowly start adding the whole wheat flour. When the dough is stiff enough to handle, turn onto a floured board and knead until dough is smooth and elastic. Place in an oiled bowl, cover and let rise until double the bulk. Knead and let rise again. Shape into two loaves; put into greased 9 × 5-inch (23 × 13 cm) loaf pans and let rise again until doubled. Bake at 400 °F (200 °C) for 45 minutes or until golden brown and the loaf sounds hollow when tapped with the fingers. Remove from pan and cool on wire racks.

Makes 2 loaves.

Calories per serving: approximately 90.

Dilly Casserole Bread

1 pkg active dry yeast
¼ c warm water (60 ml)
1 c large curd creamed cottage cheese
  (240 ml)
2 Tbsp sugar (30 ml)
1 Tbsp instant minced onion (15 ml)
1 Tbsp butter or margarine (15 ml)
2 tsp dill seeds (10 ml)
1 tsp salt (5 ml)
¼ tsp soda (1 ml)
1 egg, beaten
2¼ - 2½ c sifted all-purpose flour (540 ml)

Sprinkle yeast over warm water; stir to dissolve. Heat cottage cheese to lukewarm; combine in mixing bowl with sugar, onion, butter, dill seeds, salt, soda, egg and yeast. Add flour a little at a time, to make a stiff batter, beating well after each addition. Cover and let rise in warm place until doubled, 50 to 60 minutes. Stir down with 25 vigorous strokes. Turn into well-greased, 1½ quart (1½ liter) round casserole.

Cover and let rise in warm place 30 to 40 minutes or until almost doubled. Bake in a 350 °F (175 °C) oven for 40 to 50 minutes, until bread is a rich brown color and sounds hollow when lightly tapped with the fingers. Cover with foil the last 15 minutes to prevent excessive browning, if necessary. Remove from pan and cool on wire rack.

Makes 1 loaf.

Calories per serving: approximately 110.

Last Loaf of Summer

This is an example of the type of bread made when the kitchen at a summer cabin is cleaned up and closed at the end of the season. Any combination of grains can be used, but this is what we had on hand. The only thing to remember is that at least ⅓ of the flour used should be an all-purpose wheat flour.

2 envelopes active dry yeast
2 c warm water (480 ml)
¼ c molasses (60 ml)
2 eggs, beaten
1 Tbsp salt (15 ml)
⅓ c oil (80 ml)
1 c dry milk powder (240 ml)
½ c quick cooking oats (120 ml)
½ c yellow cornmeal (120 ml)
½ c wheat germ (120 ml)
1 c rye flour (240 ml)
2 c whole wheat flour (480 ml)
3 c all-purpose flour (720 ml)

Dissolve yeast in warm water; add molasses, stir and let stand for 2 minutes. Add beaten eggs, salt, oil, milk, oats, cornmeal and wheat germ and combine with yeast mixture in a large bowl. Add rye, whole wheat and all-purpose flour to make a soft dough. Add more all-purpose flour if necessary. Turn out on lightly floured surface and knead until smooth, about 10 minutes. Place in buttered bowl, butter surface of dough. Cover and let rise until double in bulk. Punch dough down; knead a few times, cover and allow to rest 10 minutes. Shape into two loaves and place in two greased 9 × 5 × 3-inch (23 × 13 × 8 cm) pans. Cover and let rise until double and bake at 375°F (185°C) for 20 minutes; reduce temperature to 350°F (175°C) and continue to bake for 20 minutes or until done.

Makes 2 loaves.

Calories per serving: approximately 120.

Peasant Bread

2 pkg active dry yeast
½ c warm water (120 ml)
2 c warm water (480 ml)
3 c unsifted rye flour (720 ml)
1½ tsp salt (7 ml)
2 Tbsp molasses (30 ml)
2 c mashed potatoes (480 ml)
2 Tbsp caraway or dill seeds (30 ml)
4 c unsifted all-purpose flour, approximately
  (960 ml)

Dissolve yeast in ½ c (120 ml) warm water. Add remaining water, half the rye flour, salt, molasses, potatoes and caraway or dill seeds. Blend together. Stir in white flour. Add enough rye flour so that dough is stiff enough to be kneaded. Turn out on floured board and knead well, kneading in the remaining rye flour and additional white flour if necessary to make smooth and elastic. (This is a large quantity of dough and may require a bit more kneading than most doughs.) Let rise to double in bulk (30 to 40 minutes). Punch down and divide in half. Knead again for 2 to 3 minutes. Shape and place in two 9 × 5-inch (23 × 13 cm) loaf pans or two 9-inch (23 cm) rounds or casseroles which have been greased. Allow to rise until double in bulk. Bake at 425 °F (215 °C) for 10 minutes, then lower heat to 375 °F (185 °C) and bake about 30 to 40 minutes or until done. To obtain a softer crust, brush loaves with glaze 10 minutes before end of baking time. GLAZE: Bring 1 cup (240 ml) water and 1 tablespoon (15 ml) cornstarch to a boil. Brush cornstarch mixture on loaves. Remove from pans and cool on wire rack.

Makes 2 loaves.

Calories per serving: approximately 75.

Doris Brown Heritage's Zucchini Bread

3 eggs
1 c oil (240 ml)
2 c sugar (480 ml)
2 c grated peeled zucchini (480 ml)
1 Tbsp vanilla (15 ml)
1 tsp soda (5 ml)
4 tsp baking powder (20 ml)
½ c chopped nuts (120 ml)
3 c sifted flour (720 ml)
1 tsp salt (5 ml)

Beat eggs until very light. Add sugar, oil, zucchini and vanilla. Mix lightly. Add dry ingredients which have been sifted together. Mix until well blended. Add nuts and stir. Bake in well-greased loaf pans 9 × 5 × 2 inches (23 × 13 × 5 cm) at 325°F (165°C) for 1 hour or until done.

Makes 2 loaves.

Calories per serving: approximately 125.

Doris Brown Heritage is world champion long distance runner.

Creamy Buttermilk Wheat Bread

2 envelopes active dry yeast
½ c very warm water (120 ml)
¼ c honey (60 ml)
2 c buttermilk (480 ml)
2 Tbsp shortening (30 ml)
1 Tbsp salt (15 ml)
3½ c whole wheat flour (840 ml)
½ c wheat germ (120 ml)
1 c cracked wheat or bulgur (240 ml)
2 c sifted all-purpose flour (480 ml)

Dissolve yeast in warm water; add 1 teaspoon honey and stir until yeast dissolves. Set aside until foamy, about 15 minutes. Heat buttermilk, shortening, remaining honey and salt to lukewarm and combine with yeast mixture in a large bowl. Stir in whole wheat flour, wheat germ and cracked wheat until smooth; beat in enough all-purpose flour so that a soft dough is formed. Knead until smooth and elastic. Place in lightly buttered bowl; oil top of dough. Cover and let rise until double in bulk. Punch dough down; knead a few times on lightly floured surface, cover and allow to rest 10 minutes. Form two loaves and place each in loaf pan about 9 × 5 × 3-inches (23 × 13 × 7 cm). Let rise again until double in bulk. Bake at 375°F (185°C) for 35 minutes, or until golden brown.

Makes 2 loaves.

Calories per serving: approximately 125.

Banana Nut bread

¾ c brown sugar (180 ml)
½ c margarine (120 ml)
2 eggs
1 c all-purpose flour (240 ml)
1 c whole wheat or graham flour (240 ml)
1 tsp baking soda (5 ml)
½ tsp salt (3 ml)
1 c chopped nuts (240 ml)
1 c mashed bananas (240 ml)
1 Tbsp lemon juice (15 ml)

Cream sugar and margarine until light and fluffy; add eggs and beat. Stir flours, soda, salt and nuts together until well blended and nuts are covered with flour. Combine bananas and lemon juice; add alternately with flour mixture to creamed mixture. Stir only until flour is moistened. Spread batter in a greased 9 × 5-inch (23 × 13 cm) loaf pan. Bake 1 hour at 350°F (175°C) or until toothpick comes out clean. Cool 10 minutes in pan on rack, remove and cool completely.

Makes 1 loaf.

Calories per serving: approximately 210.

Phoenix Sunflower Seed Bread

3 c sifted all-purpose flour (720 ml)
1 c sugar (240 ml)
1 tsp salt (5 ml)
3½ tsp baking powder (17 ml)
1 egg, beaten
¾ c orange juice (180 ml)
4 tsp grated orange peel (20 ml)
¾ c milk (180 ml)
¼ c butter, softened (60 ml)
¾ c roasted sunflower seeds (180 ml)

Sift dry ingredients together. Combine egg, orange juice, peel, milk and butter; add to dry ingredients, mixing well. Stir in sunflower seeds. Pour into greased 9 × 5 × 2-inch (23 × 13 × 8 cm) pan and bake at 350°F (175°C) for 1 hour. Cool on rack 15 minutes before removing from pan.

Makes 1 loaf.

Calories per serving: approximately 210.

Oatmeal Nut Bread

2 c sifted all-purpose flour (480 ml)
½ c sugar (120 ml)
2½ tsp baking powder (13 ml)
1 tsp salt (5 ml)
½ tsp soda (3 ml)
1 c rolled oats (240 ml)
1¼ c sour milk or buttermilk (300 ml)
1 egg
2 Tbsp shortening, melted (30 ml)
1 c diced, cooked prunes (240 ml)
½ c chopped nuts (120 ml)

Sift flour, sugar, baking powder, salt and soda together. Mix in rolled oats. Combine milk, egg and melted shortening. Stir the liquid into the dry ingredients. Add prunes and nuts, stirring just enough to moisten the dry ingredients. Turn into a well-greased loaf pan. Top with halved prunes and pecan halves, if desired. Bake at 350°F (175°C) for 1 hour or until done.

Makes 1 loaf.

Calories per serving: approxiamtely 160.

Pumpkin Bread

1½ c sugar (360 ml)
½ c oil (120 ml)
2 eggs, beaten
1 c pumpkin (240 ml)
⅓ c water (80 ml)
2 c unsifted all-purpose flour (480 ml)
1 tsp soda (5 ml)
1 tsp salt (5 ml)
½ tsp allspice (3 ml)
½ tsp cinnamon (3 ml)
½ tsp cloves (3 ml)
½ tsp nutmeg (3 ml)
¼ tsp baking powder (2 ml)
½ c raisins (120 ml)

Mix sugar and oil. Add eggs, pumpkin and water. Sift dry ingredients together; add to pumpkin mixture. Blend well. Stir in raisins. Pour into 9 × 5-inch (23 × 13 cm) pan. Bake at 350°F (175°C) for 1 hour or until it tests done. Remove from pan and cool on wire rack.

Makes 1 loaf.

Calories per serving: approximately 200.

Shani's Mother's Muffins

1 c 100% bran flakes (240 ml)
¼ c plus 2 Tbsp all-bran (90 ml)
1 c boiling water (240 ml)
½ c oil (120 ml)
2 eggs
2½ tsp soda (13 ml)
½ tsp salt (3 ml)
1¼ c sugar (300 ml)
2½ c flour (600 ml)
2 c buttermilk (480 ml)

Pour boiling water on bran flakes and all-bran and soak. Combine oil, eggs, soda, salt, sugar, flour and buttermilk with bran. Spoon into muffin tins and bake at 400 °F (200 °C) for 20 - 25 minutes. This recipe can successfully be doubled or tripled and will keep in the refrigerator for several weeks. Raisins may be added if desired.

Makes 24 muffins.

Calories per serving: approximately 160.

Wheat and Raisin Muffins

1 c sifted all-purpose flour (240 ml)
1 c whole wheat flour (240 ml)
2 tsp baking powder (10 ml)
1 tsp salt (5 ml)
¼ c light raisins (60 ml)
¼ c honey (60 ml)
1 egg
1 c milk (240 ml)
¼ c oil (60 ml)

Place all-purpose flour, whole wheat flour, baking powder and salt in a bowl. Mix thoroughly. Add raisins and toss gently until coated with flour. In a separate bowl, beat honey, egg, milk and oil until blended. Pour into flour mixture and stir just until blended, about 35 strokes. Place in greased muffin tins and bake at 400 °F (200 °C) for 25 minutes or until done.

Makes about 12 muffins.

Calories per serving: approximately 175.

New England Whole Wheat Maple Ring

2 pkgs active dry yeast
½ c warm water (120 ml)
¾ c milk (80 ml)
¼ c vegetable oil (60 ml)
½ c honey (120 ml)
2 tsp salt (10 ml)
2 eggs, beaten
3 c all-purpose flour (720 ml)
½ tsp nutmeg (3 ml)
2 c whole wheat flour (480 ml)
2 Tbsp melted margarine (30 ml)
½ c brown sugar (120 ml)
½ c chopped pecans (120 ml)
1 Tbsp cinnamon (15 ml)
1 tsp maple flavoring (5 ml)

Dissolve yeast in warm water; scald milk, cool and add to yeast. Add oil, honey, salt and beaten eggs to yeast mixture. Stir ⅔'s of the all-purpose flour and nutmeg together and add to liquid mixture, beating 2 minutes with an electric mixer or 5 minutes by hand. Add ½ of the whole wheat flour and beat 1 minute more. Let mixture rest for 5 minutes. Add the rest of the whole wheat flour and enough all-purpose flour to make a soft dough, mixing by hand. Turn out on lightly floured surface and knead until smooth and elastic. Place in oiled bowl; oil top of dough. Cover and let rise until double in bulk. Punch dough down; knead a few times and let rest for 10 minutes. Divide dough in half; roll into 8 × 15-inch (20 × 40 cm) rectangles and brush with melted margarine. Stir brown sugar, pecans, cinnamon and maple flavoring together; sprinkle half of the mixture evenly over each rectangle of dough. Roll each rectangle up, sealing edges, forming into a ring. Place on greased baking sheet. Cut through ring almost to the center with scissors, in slices about 1-inch (2½ cm) thick. Turn each slice slightly. Brush with melted margarine. Let rise about 30 - 45 minutes. Bake at 350 °F (175 °C) for 20 - 25 minutes; remove from oven and brush with butter or glaze.

Makes 2 rings.

Calories per serving: approximately 140.

Apple-Orange Bread

2 large oranges
1 c raisins (240 ml)
2 c applesauce (480 ml)
2 eggs, well beaten
½ c oil (120 ml)
4 c sifted all-purpose flour (960 ml)
4 tsp baking powder (20 ml)
1½ tsp salt (7 ml)
2 c sugar (180 ml)
1 c chopped nuts (240 ml)

Cut oranges in quarters. Using a medium blade, grind oranges and raisins with a food chopper. Add applesauce, eggs and oil and mix. Set aside. Combine flour, baking powder, salt, sugar, and nuts. Add to moist ingredients and stir until blended. Pour into two 8 × 5-inch (20 × 13 cm) loaf pans and bake at 350 °F (175 °C) for about 1 hour or until done.

Makes 2 loaves.

Calories per serving: approximately 175.

Alfalfa-Lemon Bread

1 c sugar (240 ml)
½ c oil (120 ml)
2 eggs
1 Tbsp lemon rind (15 ml)
1½ c all-purpose flour (360 ml)
2 tsp baking powder (10 ml)
½ tsp salt (3 ml)
⅛ tsp ginger (1 ml)
1 c alfalfa sprouts, packed (240 ml)
½ c walnuts, chopped (120 ml)

Beat sugars, oil, eggs and lemon rind. Add flour, baking powder, salt, ginger and alfalfa sprouts. Beat well. Stir in nuts. Bake in a greased 9 × 5-inch (25 × 13 cm) loaf pan at 375 °F (185 °C) for 50 - 55 minutes or until done. Cool on wire rack. This bread slices better if wrapped and stored overnight.

Makes 1 loaf.

Calories per serving: approximately 170.

Whole Wheat Biscuits

1 c sifted all-purpose flour (240 ml)
2 tsp baking powder (10 ml)
1 tsp salt (5 ml)
1 c unsifted whole wheat flour (240 ml)
¼ c shortening (60 ml)
¾ c milk (180 ml)

Sift together all-purpose flour, baking powder and salt. Add whole wheat flour and stir to mix. Cut in shortening until mixture resembles coarse meal. Make a hollow in mixture and stir in enough milk to make a soft dough. Turn onto lightly floured surface and knead 15 times. Roll to ½-inch (1 cm) thick. Cut with 2-inch (5 cm) cutter. Bake at 450°F (230°C) for 10 - 12 minutes. Serve at once.

Makes 12 - 16 biscuits.

Calories per serving: approximately 125.

County Fair Scones

1 c whole wheat flour (240 ml)
1 c all-purpose flour (240 ml)
1 Tbsp baking powder (15 ml)
⅓ c brown sugar (80 ml)
1 tsp cinnamon (5 ml)
¼ tsp salt (1 ml)
⅓ c shortening (8 ml)
½ c raisins (120 ml)
1 egg
⅔ c milk (160 ml)

Stir flours, baking powder, brown sugar, cinnamon and salt together in a bowl. Cut shortening into flour mixture until it resembles coarse crumbs. Add raisins and mix to coat. Beat egg with milk. Add to flour mixture and stir to form a soft dough. Knead lightly. Form dough into a ½-inch thick round on greased cookie sheet; cut 8 wedges. Bake at 400°F (200°C) for 15 minutes or until well done. Break apart and serve hot with butter, jam or honey.

Makes 8 scones.

Calories per serving: approximately 260.

Basketball has become the sport of the tall and lean. Players seldom worry about extra pounds! In fact, they often lose weight toward the end of the season because they don't eat enough to supply all the calories they use on the floor and under the boards. For basketball stars, from junior high to pro, desserts are more than fun... they're a tempting way to keep the pounds on.

Any meal for a basketball player should be eaten at least four hours before game or practice time. This allows time for the stomach to empty so the body can concentrate on the physical work of participating in the sport. High carbohydrate meals are recommended before games...they're easy to digest and they provide a fast source of energy.

Lots of fluids, sipped frequently but no more than two or three ounces at a time, should be available during the game. Twenty minutes before the game, a small can of grape, apple or orange juice is a quick energy booster. Orange sections and small amounts of liquids at halftime will replace the sodium, potassium and part of the liquid lost in sweat.

The following desserts will make a rich, memorable ending for a game or an all-out practice...or the perfect crowning glory to the victory meal!

Awards Night Dessert Party

Alice Browne's Carrot Cake**
Franco Columbo's Sardinian Cheese Cake**
  with fresh berries
Jefferson Davis Pie** with sour cream
Julie Hansen's Cream Cheese Ice Cream**
Assorted Cookies
Pineapple Smash*
Tea
Coffee

Recipes from basketball players:

Dave Cowens' Baked Chicken Breasts*
  Player for the Boston Celtics

"Geese" Ausbie's Lasagna*
  Player for the Harlem Globetrotters

**In this chapter
*See Index

Banana Squares

¼ c butter (60 ml)
¾ c sugar (180 ml)
1 egg
¼ c sour cream (60 ml)
½ tsp salt (3 ml)
½ tsp baking soda (3 ml)
½ tsp vanilla (3 ml)
2 small bananas, mashed
1 c sifted all-purpose flour (240 ml)

Cream butter, sugar and egg until light and fluffy. Add sour cream, salt, baking soda, vanilla, bananas and sifted flour. Mix well. Place in greased 9-inch (23 cm) square pan. Bake at 350 °F (175 °C) for 30 minutes or until done. Cool and top with Cream Cheese Frosting.

Cream Cheese Frosting

3 oz cream cheese (90 g)
3 Tbsp softened butter or margarine (45 ml)
½ tsp vanilla (3 ml)
1½ c powdered sugar (360 ml)

Blend together cream cheese, butter, vanilla and powdered sugar. Beat until light and fluffy. Spread on top of cooled banana squares.

Makes 9 servings.

Calories per serving: approximately 450.

Alice Browne's Carrot Cake

4 eggs
2 c sugar (480 ml)
1⅓ c oil (320 ml)
2 c all-purpose flour (480 ml)
2 tsp baking powder (10 ml)
2 tsp baking soda (10 ml)
2 tsp cinnamon (10 ml)
4 c grated carrots (960 ml)
1 c chopped walnuts (240 ml)

Mix eggs, sugar and oil together well. Add flour, baking powder, soda and cinnamon. Stir in carrots and walnuts. Bake in a 13 × 9 × 2-inch (33 × 23 × 5 cm) pan at 350 °F (175 °C) for 35 - 40 minutes or until done. Frost.

Frosting

8 oz cream cheese (225 g)
½ c butter or margarine (120 ml)
2 c powdered sugar (480 ml)
1 tsp vanilla (5 ml)

Blend softened cream cheese and butter together. Stir in powdered sugar and vanilla. Use to frost carrot cake.

Makes 12 servings.

Calories per serving: approximately 460.

Alice Browne is world class swimmer with the Mission Viejo Nadadores.

Orange Praline Cake

1 pkg (2 layer) yellow cake mix
2 eggs
1⅓ c orange juice (320 ml)
1½ c drained crushed pineapple (360 ml)
1 c flaked coconut (240 ml)
½ c brown sugar (120 ml)
½ c chopped pecans (120 ml)
¼ c butter, melted (60 ml)
2 c heavy cream (480 ml)
1 Tbsp sugar (15 ml)

Beat together contents of yellow cake mix, eggs and orange juice for 2 minutes. Add well drained pineapple and gently mix. Pour into 2 9-inch greased and floured cake pans and bake in a 350°F (175°C) oven for 25 - 30 minutes or until done. Mix together coconut, brown sugar, pecans and butter. Spread on 1 layer and bake an additional 10 minutes. Remove from pans and cool thoroughly. Whip cream and sugar until stiff; spread about ¼ of cream on top of praline layer. Top with additional cake layer. Use rest of whipped cream to frost top and sides of cake. Refrigerate overnight before serving.

Makes 12 servings.

Calories per serving: approximately 440.

Julie Hansen's Cream Cheese Ice Cream

½ envelope unflavored gelatin
1½ c sugar (360 ml)
1 c pineapple juice (240 ml)
1 c orange juice (240 ml)
3 Tbsp lemon juice (45 ml)
8 oz. cream cheese, softened (225 g)
¼ tsp salt (2 ml)
½ tsp almond extract (3 ml)
1 c whipping cream, whipped (240 ml)

Combine gelatin and sugar in saucepan. Add pineapple juice and heat, stirring until gelatin and sugar dissolve. Remove from heat, add orange and lemon juice. Cool. Blend cheese and salt and gradually beat in juice mixture and almond extract. Fold in whipped cream. Pour into a 2 quart (2 liter) container; freeze 6-8 hours.

Makes 2 quarts.

Calories per serving: approximately 180.

Julie Hansen competes in U.S. Olympic Discus.

Peach Cake Roll

½ c all-purpose flour (120 ml)
½ tsp baking powder (3 ml)
¼ tsp salt (1 ml)
¼ tsp cream of tartar (1 ml)
4 large eggs, separated
¾ c sugar (180 ml)
½ tsp vanilla (3 ml)
2 Tbsp powdered sugar (30 ml)
1 c cottage cheese (240 ml)
3 oz cream cheese (85 g)
¼ c sugar (60 ml)
1 Tbsp brandy or orange liqueur (15 ml)
1 Tbsp lemon juice (15 ml)
1 Tbsp grated lemon peel (15 ml)
2 c thinly sliced ripe peaches (480 ml)

Sift together flour, baking powder, and salt. Set aside. Beat egg whites and cream of tartar until foamy. Slowly add sugar and continue beating until stiff peaks are present. Beat egg yolks and vanilla until thick and lemon colored. Gently fold in beaten egg whites and flour mixture. Spoon into a shallow baking pan 10 × 15 × 1-inch (25 × 38 × 2 cm) lined with waxed paper. Bake at 375 °F (185 °C) for 10 - 12 minutes. Loosen cake from pan and trim off edges. Remove waxed paper and place on towel dusted with powdered sugar. Starting at narrow end, roll towel and cake together. Cool. Sieve cottage cheese and blend with cream cheese, sugar, brandy, lemon juice and lemon peel. When cake is cool, unroll and spread filling over cake. Arrange peaches on filling and roll back up. Chill several hours before serving. May be garnished with powdered sugar, additional fruit and sprigs of mint, if so desired.

Makes about 8 servings.

Calories per serving: approximately 250.

Pumpkin Cake

1⅔ c flour (400 ml)
1⅓ c sugar (320 ml)
½ tsp baking powder (3 ml)
1 tsp soda (5 ml)
¾ tsp salt (4 ml)
½ tsp cinnamon (2 ml)
¼ tsp cloves (1 ml)
⅓ c margarine, softened (80 ml)
2 eggs
⅓ c water (80 ml)
½ c nut meats (120 ml)
1 c pumpkin (240 ml)
⅔ c raisins (160 ml)

Sift together flour, sugar, baking powder, soda, salt, cinnamon and cloves. Add margarine and eggs. Mix well. Stir in water, nut meats, pumpkin and raisins. Mix well and bake in greased loaf pan at 350°F (175°C) for 45 minutes or until done. Let cool and frost.

Makes 1 cake.

Buttermilk Icing

1 c sugar (240 ml)
½ c buttermilk (120 ml)
½ tsp soda (3 ml)
1 Tbsp white Karo syrup (15 ml)
¼ c butter (60 ml)
1 tsp vanilla (5 ml)

Combine all ingredients except vanilla and bring to a boil. Boil to the soft ball stage, about 5 minutes. Add vanilla. Remove from heat and let cool. Beat by hand until thick enough to spread. Use to frost pumpkin cake.

Calories per serving: approximately 445.

Pineapple-Apricot Upside-Down Cake

¼ c butter or margarine (60 ml)
½ c firmly packed brown sugar (120 ml)
6 pineapple slices, drained
1 c canned apricot halves, drained
¼ c raisins (60 ml)
1¼ c sifted all-purpose flour (300 ml)
2 tsp baking powder (10 ml)
¼ tsp salt (1 ml)
1 c sugar (240 ml)
¼ c oil (60 ml)
¾ c milk (180 ml)
1 tsp vanilla (5 ml)
1 egg

Melt butter or margarine; pour into a 9 × 9 × 2-inch (23 × 23 × 5 cm) baking pan. Sprinkle brown sugar over butter. Arrange pineapple slices and apricot halves in butter-sugar mixture; fill centers of pineapple slices with raisins. Sift flour, baking powder, salt and sugar into large bowl. Add oil, milk, vanilla and egg; beat 4 - 5 minutes with electric mixer. Pour over the fruit in baking pan. Bake at 350°F (175°C) for 45 minutes, or until center springs back when lightly pressed with fingertip. Invert cake on serving plate; leave baking pan in place 2 minutes. Lift off pan. Serve warm with whipped cream, ice cream or dessert topping.

Makes 9 servings.

Calories per serving: approximately 360.

Raisin-Stuffed Apples

4 large baking apples
¼ c brown sugar (60 ml)
½ c seedless raisins, or pitted dates (120 ml)
2 Tbsp butter (30 ml)
½ c water (120 ml)

Core apples, mix brown sugar and raisins or dates and place about 2 Tbsp (30 ml) in center of each apple. Dot with butter. Place apples in large saucepan, add water and cover tightly. Bring to boil and then simmer 15 minutes, or until tender. Serve warm.

Serves 4.

Calories per serving: approximately 195.

Franco Columbu's Sardinian Cheese Cake

2 Tbsp softened butter (30 ml)
10 graham crackers
1 c sugar (240 ml)
2 lb ricotta (1 kg)
¼ c whole wheat flour (60 ml)
½ c heavy cream (120 ml)
2 Tbsp lemon juice (15 ml)
1 tsp lemon rind (5 ml)
1 tsp vanilla (5 ml)
4 eggs, well beaten

Butter bottom and sides of pan. Roll graham crackers into fine crumbs and mix with ¼th of the sugar. Cover bottom and sides of pan with crumbs, saving 2 Tbsp (30 ml) for the top. Combine remaining ingredients and rest of sugar. Beat well and pour into prepared pan. Sprinkle top with remaining crumbs. Bake in slow oven (275°F, 135°C) for 1 hour or until cake is firm in center. Allow to cool and refrigerate for at least 4 hours before serving.

Makes 18 servings.

Calories per serving: approximately 450.

Franco Columbu is an internationally known body builder.

Microwave Cheese Cake for Champions

Crust:

32 graham crackers, crushed
¼ c sugar (60 ml)
6 Tbsp butter, melted (90 ml)

Filling:

4 eggs, separated
½ c sugar (120 ml)
12 oz cream cheese (340 g)
2 tsp vanilla (10 ml)

Topping:

2 c sour cream (480 ml)
3 Tbsp sugar (45 ml)
1 tsp almond extract (5 ml)
½ tsp ground cinnamon (3 ml)

Mix graham cracker crumbs, sugar and butter; press evenly into a 7 × 11-inch (18 × 28 cm) or 10-inch (25 cm) glass pan. Refrigerate. Separate eggs and beat egg yolks until light and fluffy. Add sugar and blend well. Beat in softened cream cheese, one-fourth at a time. Blend in vanilla. In separate bowl, beat egg whites until stiff, then fold egg whites into cream cheese mixture. Blend well and turn into shell. Cook in center of microwave oven 6 minutes on high speed rotating the dish half a turn every 2 minutes. Cool 45 minutes. Blend sour cream, sugar and almond extract. Spread over cooled filling. Sprinkle with cinnamon, cook 2 minutes, rotating half a turn each minute. Cool to room temperature and place in refrigerator to chill before serving.

Serves 8.

Calories per serving: approximately 580.

Pastry and Variations

Single Crust Pie

⅔ c flour (160 ml)
½ tsp salt (2 ml)
3 Tbsp and 1 tsp shortening (50 ml)
2 Tbsp cold water (30 ml)

Double Crust Pie

1⅓ c flour (320 ml)
1 tsp salt (5 ml)
5 Tbsp and 1 tsp shortening (85 ml)
¼ c cold water (60 ml)

Combine flour and salt in medium size bowl. Cut in shortening until mixture resembles coarse cornmeal. Sprinkle water over flour mixture. Toss with fork until mixture begins to stick together. Form dough into ball. (Divide dough for double crust pies into two portions.) On lightly floured board roll dough into a circle slightly less than ⅛-inch (0.3 cm) thick, making sure diameter of circle is at least 2-inches (5 cm) larger than that of the pan. Fit dough loosely into pan. FOR SINGLE CRUST PIE: Leave at least ½-inch (1 cm) overhang. Trim away excess pastry. Fold overhang under and crimp crust. FOR DOUBLE CRUST PIE: Trim away excess pastry leaving ½-inch (1 cm) beyond the edge of pie pan. Roll remaining portion of dough to approximately the same thickness as the bottom crust. Fill bottom crust with filling. Moisten edges of bottom pastry with water. Place top crust over the bottom crust. Cut off excess pastry of top crust leaving ¾-inch (2 cm) overhang. Tuck overhang of top crust under moistened edge of bottom crust for better seal. Crimp edges of pastry.

Calories per serving: approximately 130 for single crust, approximately 164 for double crust.

Whole Wheat Pastry

½ c whole wheat pastry flour (120 ml)
½ c all-purpose flour (20 ml)
½ tsp salt (2 ml)
5 Tbsp fat (75 ml)
2 Tbsp cold water (30 ml)

Prepare in the same manner as standard pastry.

Makes 1 pastry shell.

Calories per serving: approximately 164.

Oil Pastry

1 c flour (240 ml)
½ tsp salt (2 ml)
¼ c salad oil (60 ml)
2 Tbsp milk (30 ml)

Sift flour and salt into bowl. Add oil to milk. Pour liquids into flour and stir until a ball of dough forms. Roll out as you would regular pastry or roll between 2 sheets of waxed paper.

Makes 1 pastry shell.

Calories per serving: approximately 130.

Rich Butter Pastry

1 c flour (240 ml)
2 Tbsp sugar (30 ml)
½ tsp salt (3 ml)
1 egg yolk
1 Tbsp lemon juice (15 ml)
6 Tbsp butter or margarine (90 ml)
1 Tbsp water (15 ml)

Mix flour, sugar and salt. Add egg yolk and lemon juice; mix lightly with fork. Add butter and work into dough with fingers. Add water only if needed and work dough until it forms a ball. Refrigerate dough ½ hour. Form into 6 balls and roll out each on lightly floured board to desired thickness. Bake at 400°F (200°C) for 7 minutes.

Makes 6 3-inch tart shells.

Calories per serving: approximately 220.

Deep-Dish Streusel Apple Pie

1 qt peeled and sliced tart apples (1 liter)
⅓ c granulated sugar (80 ml)
½ c raisins (120 ml)
2 tsp flour (10 ml)
½ tsp cinnamon (3 ml)
¼ tsp nutmeg (2 ml)
1 c flour (240 ml)
½ c brown sugar (120 ml)
¼ tsp salt (2 ml)
½ c butter (120 ml)

In a large bowl combine apples, granulated sugar, raisins, 2 tsp flour, cinnamon and nutmeg. Spoon into bottom of a 2 qt (2 liter) casserole. In a medium bowl combine 1 c (240 ml) flour, brown sugar and salt. Cut in butter coarsely. Sprinkle mixture over apples in casserole. Bake, uncovered, at 375°F (185°C) for 10 minutes. Reduce oven temperature to 350°F (175°C) and bake for 30 minutes longer or until topping is golden brown.

Makes 6 servings.

Calories per serving: approximately 380.

Orange Raisin Apple Pie

Pastry for single crust pie*
4 apples, sliced and peeled
½ c raisins (120 ml)
¾ c sugar (180 ml)
3 Tbsp flour (45 ml)
2½ Tbsp orange juice concentrate (40 ml)
2 tsp grated orange rind (10 ml)
2 tsp margarine (10 ml)
1 c flour (240 ml)
½ tsp cinnamon (3 ml)
½ c brown sugar (120 ml)
6 Tbsp margarine (90 ml)

Prepare pastry for single-crust pie. Combine apples, raisins, sugar, 3 Tbsp flour, orange juice and orange rind and place in pie shell. Dot with 2 tsp margarine. For streusel topping, combine 1 c flour, cinnamon and brown sugar. Cut in remaining margarine with pastry blender until mixture resembles coarse cornmeal. Sprinkle streusel topping over filling. Bake at 375°F (185°C) for 30-35 minutes or until fruit is tender.

Makes 1 pie.

Calories per serving: approximately 430.

*See index.

Cherry Cream Pie

1 c flour (240 ml)
½ c finely chopped nuts (120 ml)
¼ c packed brown sugar (60 ml)
¼ c coconut (60 ml)
½ c butter or margarine, softened (20 ml)
8 oz cream cheese, softened (225 g)
½ tsp almond extract (3 ml)
1 c powdered sugar (240 ml)
21-oz can cherry pie filling (630 g)
1 c whipping cream, whipped and sweetened
  (240 ml)

Combine flour, nuts, brown sugar, coconut and butter. Place in baking pan and bake at 375°F (185°C) for 15 - 20 minutes or until golden brown. Stir once while baking. Press warm crumbs into 9 or 10-inch (25 cm) pie plate. Chill crust. In medium bowl blend cream cheese, almond extract and powdered sugar until smooth. Spread over crust. Fold pie filling into whipped cream. Spoon over cream cheese layer. Chill 1 - 2 hours before serving.

Makes 1 pie.

Calories per serving: approximately 675.

Jefferson Davis Pie

Pastry for single-crust pie*
⅓ c margarine (80 ml)
1⅓ c light brown sugar (300 ml)
4 egg yolks
2 Tbsp flour (30 ml)
1 tsp cinnamon (5 ml)
½ tsp allspice (3 ml)
1 tsp nutmeg (5 ml)
⅔ c half and half (160 ml)
⅓ c chopped dates (80 ml)
⅓ c raisins (80 ml)
⅓ c chopped nuts (80 ml)

Prepare pastry. Cream margarine and sugar. Beat in egg yolks. Combine flour with cinnamon, allspice and nutmeg and add to creamed mixture. Stir in half and half, dates, raisins and nuts. Pour into unbaked pie shell. Bake at 350°F (175°C) for 25 - 30 minutes or until filling is set.

Makes 8 servings.

Calories per serving: approximately 550.

*See index.

Rhubarb-Strawberry Crisp

1 c sugar (240 ml)
3 Tbsp cornstarch (45 ml)
3 c fresh rhubarb, sliced (720 ml)
2 c fresh strawberries, sliced
1½ c rolled oats (360 ml)
½ c brown sugar (120 ml)
¼ c melted butter (60 ml)
⅓ c flour (80 ml)
1 tsp cinnamon (5 ml)

Combine sugar and cornstarch. Add rhubarb and strawberries. Mix lightly. Pour into 8-inch baking dish. Combine rolled oats, brown sugar, butter, flour and cinnamon. Mix until it resembles crumbs. Sprinkle over fruit. Bake at 350°F (175°C) for 30 minutes or until fruit tests tender with fork.

Makes 9 servings.

Calories per serving: approximately 270.

Cheddar Fruit Cobbler

3 - 4 c sliced apples, pears or peaches
  (750 - 1000 ml)
1 c sugar (240 ml)
2 Tbsp cornstarch (30 ml)
1 tsp cinnamon (5 ml)
1 tsp grated lemon peel (5 ml)
¼ tsp nutmeg (2 ml)
1½ c whole wheat flour (360 ml)
1 c brown sugar (240 ml)
1 c uncooked rolled oats or granola (240 ml)
½ c grated cheddar cheese (120 ml)
½ c butter (120 ml)

Gently mix fruit, sugar, cornstarch, cinnamon, lemon peel and nutmeg; place in a buttered 10-inch (25 cm) square baking dish. Combine flour, brown sugar, oats and cheese; cut in butter until mixture is crumbly. Sprinkle over fruit. Bake at 375°F (185°C) for 40 - 50 minutes. Serve warm with sour cream or ice cream.

Serves 8.

Calories per serving: approximately 540.

Queen of Hearts Pudding

4 egg yolks
4 c milk (960 ml)
4 c bread cubes (960 ml)
¾ c sugar (180 ml)
2 Tbsp butter, melted (30 ml)
1 tsp grated lemon peel (5 ml)
1 tsp vanilla (5 ml)
½ c strawberry or raspberry preserves
  (120 ml)
4 egg whites
½ tsp vanilla (3 ml)
¼ tsp cream of tartar (1 ml)
½ c sugar (120 ml)

In large bowl, beat egg yolks and milk. Stir in bread cubes, sugar, butter, lemon peel and vanilla. Blend well, and pour into 8 ungreased custard cups or a 9 × 9-inch (23 × 23 cm) baking dish. Bake at 350°F (175°C) for 40 minutes. Remove from oven and spread preserves over pudding. Beat egg whites until soft peaks form, add vanilla and cream of tartar. Gradually add ½ cup sugar, beating until stiff peaks form. Pile egg whites over preserves, sealing to edges of dish. Return to oven and bake until light brown, 10 - 12 minutes.

Makes 8 servings.

Calories per serving: approximately 380.

Crumb Pudding

¼ c butter (60 ml)
½ c sugar (120 ml)
1 egg, beaten
½ c molasses (120 ml)
½ c buttermilk (120 ml)
½ tsp soda (3 ml)
½ c raisins (120 ml)
½ c pecans (120 ml)
¼ c all-purpose flour (60 ml)
1 tsp cinnamon (5 ml)
½ tsp ground cloves (3 ml)
4 slices whole wheat bread

Cream butter and sugar, add beaten egg, molasses, buttermilk and baking soda. Mix together flour, raisins, nuts, cinnamon and cloves. Add to creamed mixture. Tear bread into uneven pieces and add to above mixture, mixing thoroughly. Place in a lightly greased 9 × 9-inch pan and bake at 350°F (175°C) for 15 minutes. Uncover and bake 15 minutes longer or until pudding is set. Serve hot.

Makes 8 servings.

Calories per serving: approximately 285.

Strawberry Bavarian

2 c sliced and hulled fresh strawberries
   (480 ml)
1 c sugar (240 ml)
2 Tbsp lemon juice (30 ml)
1 Tbsp maraschino cherry juice (15 ml)
2 envelopes unflavored gelatin (30 ml)
½ c cold water (120 ml)
1 c cream, whipped (240 ml)

Combine strawberries, sugar, lemon and cherry juices. Mix well. Soften gelatin in water and dissolve over hot water. Stir gelatin into strawberry mixture and let stand until mixture becomes slightly thickened. Fold in whipped cream. Turn mixture into 4 cup mold (1 liter); chill several hours.

Makes 6 servings.

Calories per serving: approximately 280.

Lemon Dessert

1 c flour (240 ml)
½ c margarine (120 ml)
½ c pecans (120 ml)
8 oz cream cheese (240 g)
1 c powdered sugar (240 ml)
2 c whipped topping (480 ml)
2 3-oz pkg instant lemon pudding (180 g)
3 c milk (720 ml)

Mix flour, margarine and pecans together and press into a 9 × 13-inch (23 × 33 cm) pan. Bake at 375 °F (185 °C) for 15 minutes. Allow to cool. Mix together cream cheese and sugar. Fold in half the whipped topping and spread over crust. Prepare instant pudding with milk and spread over other 2 layers. Top with rest of whipped topping. Refrigerate until ready to serve.

Makes 12 servings.

Calories per serving: approximately 430.

Most track and field athletes are characterized by low body fat percentages and high lean body mass. Stored body fat can't be relied upon for energy...work fuel must come from a steady amount of high energy food in moderate amounts throughout the day. If energy isn't provided by food, muscles will be broken down to

do the job. High carbohydrate snacks and sandwiches can be carried to competitions or the training field...and be ready when a quick energy pick-up is needed.

Endurance athletes use stored carbohydrate or glycogen in greater amounts than field participants. They need more fruits, whole grains and vegetables such as corn, peas and squash. Increased protein is needed in severe muscular contraction so the power field athlete also requires extra protein to cover energy needs.

Timing for meals depends on training schedules. Early morning runners can drink a small can of juice, train, then have a hearty breakfast. Afternoon trainers can have bountiful breakfasts, but lunch should be small...and at least 2 hours before track time.

Fluids are a primary consideration, and should be on the field in plentiful supply in the form of oranges, water, diluted fruit juices or vegetable juices. These fluids prevent dehydration and also provide the electrolytes needed for muscular contraction.

For a quick, at-home lunch or an action-packed snack on the field, the following recipes will keep track and field athletes on the go!

Out The Door

Breakfast Bars**
Fruit juice in small cans

In the Cooler

TFS Sandwiches*
Ken Foreman's Bean Salad*
Fruits & Vegetables in Season
Stuffed Prunes**
High Energy Candy**
Apple juice

Home After the Meet

Spinach Salad*
Teresa Smith's Mexican Sunday Night Supper*
Tortillas & Corn Bread
Julie Hansen's Cream Cheese Ice Cream*
Lots of water and juice

Recipes from runners and track and field athletes:

Deanna Coleman's Oven Beef Stew*
  Record holder for 800 m and mile in high school

Darrel Corn's Potatoes*
  Record holder in Shot & Discus at Seattle Pacific University

Kenneth Foreman's Bean Salad
  U.S. Olympic Women's Track and Field Coach

Julie Hansen's Cream Cheese Ice Cream*
  U.S. Olympic Discus

Doris Brown Heritage's Zucchini Bread*
  World Record Holder in Women's Long Distance Running

Gerry Lindgren's Runners' Energy Drink**
  Former World Record Holder in 6 mile, 3 time U.S. Olympic Team runner, 11 NCAA championships in running.

Marcia Mecklenberg's Chicken with Orange Sauce*
  U.S. Indoor 2nd place in shot, 4th ranked in U.S.

Teresa Smith's Mexican Sunday Night Supper*
  U.S. Pentathlete record holder

**In this chapter
*See Index

What To Take on the Road

The following snack ideas are guaranteed to stave off hunger and provide good nutrition. Good eating will bolster confidence in any performance. If you are on your way to compete, select snacks from the asterisk* group that are easily digested.

Dairy Foods:
  small squares of Longhorn, Swiss or
  Mozzarella cheese
  cottage cheese*
  yogurt, creamy or frozen*
  low fat milk in a thermos with ice cubes
(to keep dairy products cold, chill and wrap
in several pages of newspaper)

Fruit Foods:
  apples, pears, peaches
  navel oranges, peeled and sectioned*
  Mandarin oranges, canned fruit cocktail*
  fresh berries, grapes, cantaloupe*
  bananas*
  jars of applesauce*
  canned fruit juices*
  dried fruits

Vegetable foods:
  broccoli, green beans, cauliflower pieces
  carrot sticks and celery sticks
  cherry tomatoes, peas

Meat foods:
  small meatballs
  canned tuna (water packed)
  peanut butter
  nuts
  beef jerky
  hard-cooked eggs (unpeeled)

Cereal foods:
  granola
  lightly buttered toast
  zwieback*
  wheat or oyster crackers*
  bagel and cream cheese
  cold cereals*
  canned puddings*
  breakfast bars

Stuffed Prunes

18 lg prunes, pitted
3 oz cream cheese (90 g)
¼ c sunflower seeds (60 ml)
2 tsp grated lemon peel (10 ml)

Mix together the cheese, sunflower seeds and lemon peel and stuff about 1 teaspoonful into each of the pitted prunes.

Makes 18 stuffed prunes.

Calories per serving: approximately 50.

Track Snack

1 c raisins (240 ml)
3½ oz cashew nuts (160 ml)
6 oz chocolate chips (180 g)
3½ oz peanuts, roasted with skin (160 ml)

Combine all ingredients together and store in a jar or plastic bag.

Makes about 2½ cups.

Calories per cup: approximately 950.

Stretch Jello

2 pkg unflavored gelatin (15 g)
6 oz jello, any flavor (180 g)
2½ c water (600 ml)
¼ c sugar (60 ml)

Dissolve unflavored gelatin in 1 cup cold water. Set aside. Add 1 cup boiling water to jello and sugar. Combine with gelatin, stir and add remaining ½ cup cold water. Pour into greased pan. Place in refrigerator for 2 hours or until set. Cut into 24 squares. This jello will stay solid at room temperature and can be eaten with the fingers just like candy.

Calories per serving: approximately 37.

High Energy Candy

½ c honey (120 ml)
½ c peanut butter (120 ml)
1½ c nonfat dry milk powder (360 ml)

Mix well with hands, kneading to a smooth consistency. Shape as desired and roll in either nuts, raisins, coconut, wheat germ or sesame seeds.

Makes 15 tablespoon sized pieces.

Calories per serving: approximately 150.

Toasted Pumpkin Seeds

2 c pumpkin seeds, washed (480 ml)
½ c butter, melted (120 ml)
1 tsp Tabasco sauce (5 ml)
1 tsp Worcestershire sauce (5 ml)
1 Tbsp seasoning salt (15 ml)

Soak seeds in salted water overnight. Drain and place seeds in low baking pan. Drizzle butter, Tabasco, Worcestershire and seasoning salt mixture over seeds. Bake at 300°F (150°C) for 20 minutes.

Calories per cup: approximately 805.

Corn Bread Snacks

8 oz corn muffin mix (240 g)
1 c chopped peanuts (240 ml)
¼ c grated Parmesan cheese (60 ml)
¼ c grated Cheddar Cheese (60 ml)
½ tsp garlic salt (2 ml)
½ tsp celery seed (2 ml)
3 Tbsp melted butter (45 ml)

Prepare corn bread according to package directions. Spread in 15 × 11 inch (37 × 27 cm) greased pan. Sprinkle with peanuts, Parmesan cheese, Cheddar cheese, garlic salt and celery seed. Drip melted butter on top. Bake at 350°F (175°C) for about 25 minutes or until lightly browned. Cut into squares.

Makes 20 squares.

Calories per square: approximately 90.

Mexican Popcorn

3 qts popped corn (3 liters)
¼ c butter, melted (60 ml)
1 pkg taco seasoning mix

Pour the melted butter over freshly popped, hot popcorn. Sprinkle on the taco seasoning mix. Toss the popcorn gently until it is coated evenly. Serve immediately.

Variations: try spaghetti sauce mix, salad seasoning mix, or cheese-bacon-chive dip mix.

Makes 3 quarts.

Calories per cup: approximately 100.

Cheesey Shredded Wheat

4 c spoon-sized shredded wheat (960 ml)
½ c margarine (120 ml)
1 c grated Cheddar cheese (240 ml)

Melt margarine. Place shredded wheat on cookie sheet and pour on melted margarine. Sprinkle on grated cheese. Bake at 375°F (185°C) for 10 minutes or until cheese is melted. Eat while warm.

Makes 4 cups.

Calories per cup: approximately 500.

Sunny Oatmeal Cookies

1 c butter or margarine (240 ml)
1 c brown sugar (240 ml)
1 c granulated sugar (240 ml)
2 eggs
1 tsp vanilla (5 ml)
1½ c all-purpose flour (360 ml)
¾ tsp salt (4 ml)
1 tsp soda (5 ml)
3 c quick-cooking rolled oats (720 ml)
1 c sunflower seeds (240 ml)

Cream together butter, brown sugar and granulated sugar. Add eggs, vanilla and beat to blend. Add flour, salt, soda and rolled oats. Mix. Gently blend in sunflower seeds. Form in long rolls about 1½-inches (4 cm) in diameter. Wrap in plastic film and chill. Slice ¼-inch thick. Arrange on ungreased cookie sheet and bake at 350°F (175°C) for 10 minutes, or until lightly browned.

Makes 8 dozen.

Calories per serving: approximately 60.

Salted Peanut Cookies

1 c brown sugar (240 ml)
1 c white sugar (240 ml)
1 c shortening (240 ml)
2 eggs
1 tsp baking powder (5 ml)
1 tsp soda (5 ml)
2 c all-purpose flour (480 ml)
1 c crushed corn flakes (240 ml)
1 c oatmeal (240 ml)
1 c salted peanuts (240 ml)
1 tsp vanilla (5 ml)
Sugar

Cream thoroughly sugars and shortening. Add eggs, one at a time. Sift together baking powder, soda and flour and add corn flakes, oatmeal, salted peanuts and vanilla. Roll into balls the size of a walnut; sprinkle with sugar and bake at 375°F (185°C) for about 8 minutes or until done.

Makes 3 dozen.

Calories per serving: approximately 150.

My Old Boyfriend's Favorite Oatmeal Cookie

1 c soft butter or margarine (240 ml)
1 c brown sugar (240 ml)
1 c white sugar (240 ml)
¼ c honey (60 ml)
1 c milk (240 ml)
1 tsp vanilla (5 ml)
1 egg
1 c all-purpose flour (240 ml)
⅓ c soy flour (80 ml)
2 c whole wheat flour (480 ml)
1 tsp baking soda (5 ml)
¼ tsp cloves (1 ml)
½ tsp nutmeg (3 ml)
1 tsp cinnamon (5 ml)
1 c rolled oats (240 ml)
1 c wheat germ (240 ml)
2 c raisins (480 ml)

In a large bowl beat the butter, brown sugar and white sugar until creamy. Beat in honey. Blend milk, vanilla and egg in a small bowl. Combine the all-purpose flour, soy flour, whole wheat flour, soda, cloves, nutmeg, cinnamon and add alternately with the milk mixture to the creamed butter and sugar. Stir in oats, wheat germ and raisins. Drop level teaspoonfuls about 2-inches apart on a well greased cookie sheet. Bake at 350°F (175°C) until lightly browned, about 8 minutes. Remove pan from oven. Let stand about 3 minutes, then remove cookies and cook on wire racks.

Makes about 9 dozen.

Calories per serving: approximately 40.

Chewy Peanut Bars

½ c butter (120 ml)
½ c peanut butter (120 ml)
½ c brown sugar (120 ml)
½ c honey (120 ml)
1 tsp vanilla (5 ml)
½ tsp salt (3 ml)
5 c granola (1200 ml)

Melt butter in a saucepan over low heat. Remove from heat and stir in peanut butter, brown sugar, honey, vanilla, salt and granola. Press firmly into a well greased 10 × 12-inch (25 × 32 cm) pan. Bake at 325°F (165°C) for 20-25 minutes or until cookies are light brown around edges. Remove from oven, cool and cut into bars while still warm.

Makes about 30 2" squares.

Calories per serving: approximately 90.

Keith's Cookies

1 c margarine (240 ml)
2 c brown sugar (480 ml)
1 c smooth peanut butter (240 ml)
2 eggs
¼ c milk (60 ml)
1¼ c all-purpose flour (300 ml)
1 c whole wheat flour (240 ml)
1 tsp baking soda (5 ml)
2 c chocolate chips (480 ml)
2 c chocolate chips (480 ml)

Cream margarine, sugar and peanut butter together until light and fluffy; add eggs and milk and blend. Stir flour, salt and baking soda together, add to creamed mixture. Stir in chocolate chips. Drop dough by tablespoons onto lightly greased cookie sheet. Bake 375°F (185°C) for 10-12 minutes.

Makes about 4 dozen.

Calories per serving: approximately 140.

Orange Drop Cookies

1 egg
1 c firmly packed brown sugar (240 ml)
¼ c oil (60 ml)
1½ c quick cooking rolled oats (360 ml)
1½ c Grape Nuts (360 ml)
½ c raisins (120 ml)
½ c broken walnuts (120 ml)
½ c orange juice (120 ml)
1 c sifted all-purpose flour (240 ml)
2 tsp baking powder (10 ml)
¼ tsp salt (1 ml)
¼ tsp allspice (1 ml)

Mix together egg, sugar and oil. Add oats, Grape Nuts, raisins and walnuts, stirring to mix well after each addition. Stir in orange juice. Sift remaining dry ingredients together over mixture; stir until blended. Drop by teaspoonful onto lightly greased cookie sheets. Bake at 375°F (185°C) for 8-10 minutes or until cookies are lightly browned.

Makes 4 dozen.

Calories per serving: approximately 60.

Chocolate Chip Granola Bars

½ c butter (120 ml)
½ c brown sugar (120 ml)
½ c honey (120 ml)
1 tsp vanilla (5 ml)
½ tsp salt (3 ml)
4 c granola (960 ml)
½ c coconut (120 ml)
½ c sliced almonds (120 ml)
6 oz chocolate chips (180 g)

Melt butter in large saucepan over low heat. Remove from heat and stir in brown sugar, honey, vanilla, salt, granola, coconut, nuts and chocolate chips. Stir until well-blended. Turn into a well greased 9 × 13 inch (20 × 32 cm) pan, packing firmly with hands. Bake 325°F (165C) for 20-25 minutes until cookies are bubbly. Remove from oven and cut into 30 2-inch bars. Cool.

Makes 30.

Calories per serving: approximately 100.

Helen's Carrot Cookies

½ c butter (120 ml)
1 c brown sugar (240 ml)
2 eggs
½ tsp grated orange rind (3 ml)
1½ c whole wheat flour (360 ml)
½ tsp baking soda (2 ml)
1 tsp baking powder (5 ml)
½ tsp salt (3 ml)
2 c grated carrots (480 ml)
½ c walnuts, chopped (120 ml)
½ c raisins (120 ml)

Cream butter, sugar and eggs until light and fluffy; blend in orange rind. Stir together dry ingredients and add alternately with carrots to creamed mixture. Fold in walnuts and raisins. Drop tablespoonfuls onto a greased cookie sheet and bake at 400°F (200°C) for 10-12 minutes.

Makes 36.

Calories per cookie: approximately 85.

Whole Grain Date Chews

½ c shortening (120 ml)
½ c brown sugar (120 ml)
¼ c granulated sugar (60 ml)
1 egg
1 tsp vanilla (5 ml)
1 c whole wheat flour (240 ml)
¾ tsp salt (4 ml)
1¼ tsp baking powder (6 ml)
½ c finely chopped dates (120 ml)
½ c chocolate chips (120 ml)
¾ c chopped walnuts (180 ml)

Cream shortening, brown sugar, granulated sugar, egg and vanilla until light. Add flour, salt, baking powder, dates, chocolate chips, and nuts. Stir until blended. Drop by teaspoonful onto greased cookie sheet. Bake at 375°F (185°C) for 10 minutes or until cookies are lightly browned.

Makes 3½ dozen.

Calories per serving: approximately 70.

Breakfast Bars

1 c whole wheat flour (240 ml)
½ c soy flour (120 ml)
¼ c bran (60 ml)
1 c nonfat dry milk powder (240 ml)
1 Tbsp baking powder (15 ml)
½ tsp salt (3 ml)
1 tsp cinnamon (5 ml)
½ tsp nutmeg (3 ml)
1 c walnuts (240 ml)
1 c brown sugar (240 ml)
½ c milk (120 ml)
2 c grated carrots (480 ml)

Stir whole wheat flour, soy flour, bran, dry milk, baking powder, salt, cinnamon and nutmeg together. Add nuts, brown sugar and mix well. Add eggs, oil, milk and carrots. Stir until moistened. Bake in 9 × 13 inch (20 × 32 cm) pan at 350 °F (175 °C) for 40 minutes or until done. Cut.

Makes 24 bars.

Calories per serving: approximately 180.

Beautiful Banana Stick

¼ c brown sugar (60 ml)
½ c oil (120 ml)
2 eggs
1 c mashed banana (240 ml)
1¾ c whole wheat flour (420 ml)
2 tsp baking powder (10 ml)
½ tsp baking soda (2 ml)
¼ tsp salt (1 ml)

Combine brown sugar, oil, eggs and bananas until smooth. Mix flour, baking powder, baking soda and salt and add to liquid ingredients. Mix only until smooth. Pour into greased 9 × 5 inch (20 × 12 cm) pan and bake at 350 °F (175 °C) until done, about 45 minutes. Cook and cut into slices ½-¾ inches (1-1½ cm) thick. Place on cookie sheets and bake at 105 °F (80 °C) for 3-4 hours or until chunky and dry. Store in tightly covered container.

Makes about three dozen.

Calories per serving: approximately 50.

Erik's Oatmeal Crackers

3 c old-fashioned oatmeal (720 ml)
1 c wheat germ (240 ml)
2 c whole wheat flour (480 ml)
3 Tbsp brown sugar (45 ml)
1 tsp salt (5 ml)
¾ c oil (180 ml)
1 c water (240 ml)

Combine all ingredients and roll into a very thin layer on 2 oiled cookie sheets. Cut into 2-inch squares and sprinkle with salt. Bake 30 minutes at 300 °F (150 °C).

Makes about 72 crackers.

Calories per serving: approximately 90.

Gerry Lindgren's Runners' Energy Drink

2 eggs
2 whole bananas
1 cup any kind of ice cream
1½ cups milk
Fruit to taste (anything in season: apples, pears, strawberries, etc.)

Mix all ingredients in blender at high speed, till thick and foamy. Eat with toast...great before a meet!

Makes 2 servings.

Calories per serving: approximately 660 (will vary with added fruit).

Gerry Lindgren is a 3 time U.S. Olympic team runner, former world record holder in 6 mile, and holds 11 NCAA championships in running.

Young baseball players practice early in the evening and miss mom's regular dinners. Semi-pros travel with a limited daily allowance and dine on fast foods. The professionals and their fifteen million fans spend long hot hours in the sun and don't consider a hearty meal till after the final inning...so dinner is something everyone looks forward to!

A baseball player's caloric needs aren't excessive, and stored energy will provide all he needs to perform a variety of tasks. The watch-and-wait sport requires more hand-to-eye coordination and individual skill than exhausting physical effort. The action can take forever to start...but when it does, the whole field explodes! Short, speedy runs from base to base are similar to sprints in track events. The intense work done by the pitcher and base runner is classified as anaerobic, or without oxygen.

The following quick dinner dishes will satisfy evening hunger pains of fans and players alike... and provide stored energy for a winning season! Many of the recipes can be made ahead and held until after the game is over.

After-the-Game Suppers

Home Run Stroganoff**
Minute Rice
Carrot and Peanut Salad*
Banana Squares*
Milk or Iced Tea

Recipe from a baseball player:

Hank Aaron's Shrimp Creole**
   Legendary baseball player with the Atlanta Braves

Big Sky Chili**
Fresh Vegetable Plate
Bread Sticks or Crackers
Microwave Cheesecake for Champions*
Lemonade

Favorite Fish Bake**
Fruit and Vegetable Salad*
Whole Wheat Rolls*
Chocolate Chip Granola Bars*
Milk or Spiced Tea

"Wrapped Up" Hamburger Dinner**
Garden Green Salad* with Dill Dressing*
Blueberry Shake*

**In this chapter
*See Index

Home Run Stroganoff

1½ lb lean beef stew meat (700 mg)
10½ oz condensed cream of mushroom soup
   (315 g)
½ pkg dry onion soup mix
½ c red wine or beef broth (120 ml)

Mix ingredients in a covered 2 quart (2 liter) baking dish. Bake at 250°F (115°C) for 8 hours. This can be cooked in a crock pot and will keep until after the game.

Serves 6.

Calories per serving: approximately 380.

Bill Feinberg's Flank Steak Marinade

1 flank steak
½ c soy sauce (120 ml)
2 cloves garlic, chopped
¼ c salad oil (60 ml)
2 tsp sugar (10 ml)
1 tsp ginger (5 ml)

Combine all ingredients. Pour over flank steak; marinate 4-5 hours. Broil or barbecue for 10-15 minutes over medium heat.

Serves 4.

Calories per serving: approximately 325.

Bill Feinberg is a natonally ranked table tennis champion.

Dugout Macaroni-Beef Casserole

1 c elbow macaroni (240 ml)
2 lb lean ground beef (900 g)
1 c diced onion (240 ml)
1 clove garlic, mashed
2 Tbsp oil (30 ml)
8 oz tomato sauce (220 g)
½ c catsup (120 ml)
4 diced tomatoes
4 oz sliced mushrooms (120 g)
2 tsp Worcestershire sauce (10 ml)
1 tsp salt (5 ml)
1 tsp Italian seasoning (5 ml)
Pepper to taste

Cook macaroni in boiling salted water, drain and set aside. In a large skillet, saute the ground beef, onion and garlic in oil. Discard any extra fat. Add tomato sauce, catsup, tomatoes, mushrooms, Worcestershire sauce, salt, seasoning and pepper to taste. Simmer for 10 minutes. Add cooked macaroni and simmer for 5 more minutes.

Serves 6 generously.

Calories per serving: approximately 600.

In my family we called this slum gullion, as mom would put in all the leftovers, and there was always enough for all your friends to sample.—M.S.P.

Sprinter's Meat Loaf

1 lb ground beef (450 g)
1 c alfalfa sprouts (240 ml)
2 eggs
1 onion, minced
½ c bread crumbs (120 ml)
1 tsp salt (5 ml)
¼ tsp pepper (1 ml)

Mix all ingredients together until well blended. Place mixture in a 9 × 5 inch (23 × 12 cm) loaf pan and bake and 350°F (175°C) for 1 hour. Serve warm or cold.

Serves 4-6.

Calories per serving: approximately 300.

Big Sky Chili

4 slices bacon
2 onions, chopped
4 cloves garlic, minced
3 lb lean beef stew meat (1½ kg)
4 c beef bouillon (1 liter)
2 Tbsp vinegar (30 ml)
2 Tbsp sugar (30 ml)
3 large tomatoes, peeled and chopped
2 Tbsp chili powder (30 ml)
2 bay leaves, crushed
1 tsp cumin (5 ml)
½ tsp crushed red pepper (3 ml)
2 tsp salt (10 ml)
½ tsp black pepper (3 ml)

Fry bacon, onions and garlic in pan until evenly browned. Remove from pan and brown beef. Add browned bacon mixture, bouillon, vinegar, sugar and tomatoes to beef. Simmer for 2 hours, adding a little water if necessary. Add chili powder, bay leaves, cumin, red pepper, salt and black pepper. Simmer 1 more hour, adding more liquid if necessary. Serve with beans or rice. This is even better when reheated.

Serves 8.

Calories per serving: approximately 420.

Italian Spaghetti Sauce for Norwegians

1½ lb lean ground beef (750 g)
8 oz ham, finely chopped (225 g)
2 garlic cloves, minced
½ c chopped onions (120 ml)
½ c chopped celery (120 ml)
½ c sliced carrots (120 ml)
4 oz fresh mushrooms, sliced (120 g)
1 c beef broth (240 ml)
1 Tbsp chopped parsley (15 ml)
¼ tsp nutmeg (1 ml)
1 tsp salt (5 ml)
½ tsp freshly ground pepper (3 ml)
1 Tbsp sugar (15 ml)
4 large tomatoes, diced
6 oz can tomato paste (180 ml)
½ c dry white wine (120 ml)

Fry beef in skillet until meat loses red color; discard all but 2 Tbsp (30 ml) fat. Add ham, garlic, onions, celery, carrots and mushrooms and saute for 2-3 minutes. Add broth, parsley, nutmeg, salt, pepper, sugar, tomatoes, tomato paste and wine and simmer uncovered, stirring frequently for 2-3 hours. Refrigerate until ready to serve.

Makes about 1½ quarts (1½ liters).

Calories per cup: approximately 376.

"Wrapped-Up" Hamburger Dinner

2 lb lean hamburger (900 g)
3 potatoes
3 carrots
2 zucchini
1 onion
Salt and pepper
Catsup

Make 6 hamburger patties and place each on a 12 × 12 inch (23 × 23 cm) foil square. Slice vegetables and place a portion of each on each meat patty. Sprinkle with salt and pepper and add a dollop catsup. Seal securely. These may be frozen and cooked when needed. Bake at 350°F (175°C) for 45 minutes if not frozen or for 60 minutes if frozen. These foil packages may be wrapped in newspaper to keep warm and carried to your favorite spectator sport.

Serves 6.

Calories per serving: approximately 325.

Spanish Eggs

½ lb hamburger (240 g)
½ c minced onion (120 ml)
¼ c green pepper (60 ml)
1 clove minced garlic
1 c tomato sauce (240 ml)
1 tsp salt (5 ml)
1 tsp chili powder (5 ml)
6 eggs

Saute hamburger, onion, green pepper and garlic in a skillet. Remove excess fat. Add tomato sauce, salt and chili powder. Simmer 10 minutes. Crack eggs into a bowl and lightly scramble them with a fork. While chili mixture is boiling, pour eggs on top. Do not stir until eggs are almost firm. Mix together gently and serve.

Serves 4.

Calories per serving: approximately 340.

Turkey and Ham Sports Pack

4 slices cooked ham
4 slices cooked turkey
10 oz French-style green beans (315 g)
¼ c slivered almonds (60 ml)
1 c shredded cheese (240 ml)
Salt and pepper

Place a piece of ham and a piece of turkey on each of four 12 × 12 inch (29 × 29 cm) foil squares. Divide beans, almonds, and cheese and place on top of each meat stack. Season to taste. Wrap securely and refrigerate until needed. To heat, bake at 350 °F (175 °C) for 25 to 30 minutes.

Serves 4.

Calories per serving: approximately 260.

Mixed Grill

6 lamb chops
6 strips bacon
2 thinly sliced potatoes
¼ c vegetable oil (60 ml)
Salt, pepper and garlic salt
2 thinly sliced tomatoes
Seasoned fine bread crumbs

Wrap each chop with bacon and place on broiler pan. Dip potatoes in oil, season with salt and pepper and place on pan. Broil lamb and potatoes 6 minutes on one side. Turn lamb and potatoes and season with salt, pepper and garlic salt. Dip tomatoes in oil, sprinkle with crumbs and add to the pan. Broil for 3 to 4 minutes or until desired doneness.

Serves 3.

Calories per serving: approximately 600.

Sesame Chicken

1 egg
2 Tbsp water (30 ml)
½ c flour (120 ml)
¼ c sesame seed (60 ml)
1 tsp salt (5 ml)
¼ tsp ground pepper (2 ml)
2½ lb chicken, in pieces (1 kg)
2-3 Tbsp butter (60-90 ml)

Combine the egg and water. In another dish, mix the flour, sesame seed, salt and pepper. Melt butter in a 9 inch (22 cm) baking pan. Dip chicken parts in egg mixture, then in flour mixture. Place in pan, turning so that the butter coats all sides well. Bake at 350°F (175°C) for about 45 minutes or until tender, brown and crisp. Serve warm or cold.

Serves about 4.

Calories per serving: approximately 375.

Favorite Fish Bake

11 oz frozen breaded fish squares (330 g)
10 oz frozen chopped spinach (300 g)
11 oz canned condensed Cheddar cheese soup (330 g)
2 Tbsp milk (30 ml)
¼ tsp ground nutmeg (2 ml)
¼ c wheat germ (60 ml)
¼ c bran flake cereal (60 ml)
1 Tbsp butter, melted (15 ml)

Arrange fish squares in a 9 × 9 inch (23 × 23 cm) baking dish, baking at 425°F (215°C) for 10 minutes. Defrost and drain spinach and place on top of fish. Combine cheese soup, milk and nutmeg and pour over fish. Combine the wheat germ, bran flake cereal and butter and sprinkle over top. Return to oven for 5-10 minutes or until heated throughout.

Serves 4 generously.

Calories per serving: approximately 250.

Shrimp Newburg

¼ c margarine (60 ml)
1 tsp flour (5 ml)
½ c whipping cream (120 ml)
2 egg yolks, beaten
2 Tbsp sherry (30 ml)
1 tsp finely chopped green onion (5 ml)
6 oz can shrimp, drained (180 g)
Salt and white pepper
1½ c cooked rice (360 ml)

Melt margarine in small saucepan. Stir in flour, add cream and simmer until mixture thickens. Stir sauce into beaten egg yolks. Return sauce to pan and add sherry, onion and shrimp. Season with salt and pepper and simmer until shrimp are warmed through. Serve with cooked rice.

Serves 4.

Calories per serving: approximately 380.

Western Rally Shrimp

1 c sliced mushrooms (240 ml)
2 Tbsp butter (30 ml)
2 Tbsp all-purpose flour (30 ml)
½ c milk (120 ml)
10½ oz canned cream of mushroom soup
  (315 g)
⅓ c cooking sherry (80 ml)
3 Tbsp grated Parmesan cheese (45 ml)
15 oz can artichoke hearts, drained (435 g)
14 oz cooked shrimp (410 g)
¼ c toasted slivered almonds (60 ml)

Saute mushrooms in butter. Remove mushrooms and blend in flour, and then milk. Add soup, sherry and cheese. Just before serving, stir in mushrooms, artichokes, and shrimp and simmer 5 minutes. Serve with fluffy rice, hot buttered biscuits or in patty shells, topped with almonds.

Serves 8.

Calories per serving: approximately 190.

Quick Egg Foo Yung

2 tsp soy sauce (10 ml)
1 tsp cornstarch (5 ml)
1 tsp sugar (5 ml)
1 tsp vinegar (5 ml)
¾ tsp salt (4 ml)
½ c cold water (120 ml)
1 c bean sprouts (240 ml)
⅔ c sliced onion (160 ml)
5½ oz shrimp (150 g)
6 eggs, slightly beaten
2 Tbsp oil (30 ml)
½ c chow mein noodles (120 ml)

Combine soy sauce, cornstarch, sugar, vinegar, salt and water. Stir over low heat until thickened. Combine sprouts, onion and shrimp. Add beaten eggs. Fry in oil as one large pancake, turning once. When all the mixture is cooked, cover with heated sauce and serve at once. Sprinkle with chow mein noodles.

Serves 4.

Calories per serving: approximately 300.

Clam Rarebit

6½ oz canned minced clams (200 g)
2 Tbsp minced onion (30 ml)
2 Tbsp catsup (30 ml)
Dash bottled hot pepper sauce
1 c diced Cheddar cheese (240 ml)
2 Tbsp chopped ripe olives (30 ml)
1 tsp Worcestershire sauce (5 ml)
4 slices bread, toasted

Drain claims. Mix with onions, catsup, hot pepper sauce, cheese, olives and Worcestershire sauce. Heat over low heat until cheese melts and mixture is bubbly. Pour over toasted bread.

Serves 4.

Calories per serving: approximately 300.

Ginger Beans and Franks

2 c canned pork and beans (480 ml)
½ c honey (120 ml)
¼ c chopped onion (60 ml)
½ tsp ginger (2 ml)
1 lb frankfurters (450 g)
16 oz canned sliced peaches, drained (450 g)
2 tsp grated orange rind (10 ml)
1 Tbsp sugar (15 ml)

Combine beans, honey, onion and ginger. Slice franks diagonally and add to beans. Place in 7 × 9 inch (17 × 22 cm) baking dish and top with sliced peaches. Mix orange rind and sugar and sprinkle over peaches. Bake at 325 °F (165 °C) for 45 minutes. Reheats well in a microwave.

Serves 4.

Calories per serving: approximately 650.

Brian Goodell's Red Noodles

2 Tbsp butter (30 ml)
1 chopped onion
24 oz. tomato sauce (750 ml)
1 c water (240 ml)
1 Tbsp chopped parsley (15 ml)
Salt, pepper
8 oz elbow macaroni (240 g)

Melt butter and saute onion. Add tomato sauce, water and parsley. Salt and pepper to taste. Simmer to blend flavors, about 30 minutes. Cook macaroni according to package directions. Drain and rinse. Add macaroni to sauce and serve.

Serves 4.

Calories per serving: approximately 400.

Brian Goodell is the world record holder in the 1500 meter and the 800 meter freestyle.

Baseball Franks and Corn Bake

½ c chopped green pepper (120 ml)
¼ c chopped onion (60 ml)
¼ c butter (60 ml)
2 c soft bread crumbs (480 ml)
17 oz canned cream-style corn (500 g)
12 oz can whole kernel corn, drained (360 g)
2 eggs, beaten
¼ c fine, dry bread crumbs (60 ml)
1 Tbsp butter, melted (15 ml)
1 lb frankfurters (450 g)

Saute pepper and onion in butter. Add bread crumbs, corn and eggs and mix lightly. Spoon into 9 × 9 inch (22 × 22 cm) baking dish. Combine dry bread crumbs and melted butter and sprinkle over corn mixture. Bake at 350°F (175°C) for 30 minutes. Refrigerate until ready to serve. Place franks in straight row across corn and bake for 20 minutes at 350°F (175°C) or until warm throughout.

Serves 5.

Calories per serving: approximately 550.

Kyle's Texas Tacos

1 large onion, chopped
2 Tbsp oil (30 ml)
1½ lb lean ground beef (500 g)
1 lb whole tomatoes, chopped (450 g)
½ tsp salt (3 ml)
¼ tsp cumin (1 ml)
½ tsp garlic salt (3 ml)
½ tsp chili powder (3 ml)

Saute onion in oil; add beef and brown. Drain excess fat. Add tomatoes to this mixture. Add spices according to your taste, cover and simmer for 2 hours. Stir often. Use this meat mixture in heated taco shells and garnish with chopped lettuce, tomato and grated cheese.

Makes enough for 10 taco shells.

Calories per serving: approximately 200.

Kyle Rote Jr. is a soccer player for the Dallas Tornadoes and has been an A.B.C. Super Star for several years.

Monster Man Trout

4 pan sized trout (about 10 oz or 275 g)
2 Tbsp oil (30 ml)
½ tsp seasoning salt (3 ml)
Freshly ground pepper
1 fresh lemon
Melted butter or Bearnaise sauce

Rinse trout thoroughly and pat dry with paper toweling. Brush skin with oil and season body cavity with seasoning salt and pepper. Place on a rack in a broiler pan and bake at 350 °F (175 °C) for 20 minutes or until done. Be careful not to overbake. Fish is done when it flakes when tested with a fork. Place on warm plates and serve immediately with a wedge of fresh lemon and melted butter or Bearnaise sauce.

Serves 4.

Calories per serving: approximately 300.

Hank Aaron's Shrimp Creole

½ c butter (120 ml)
1 large onion
1 medium green pepper
2 c celery (480 ml)
2 cloves garlic, minced
2½ c pureed tomatoes (600 ml)
2 c tomato sauce (480 ml)
2 Tbsp Worcestershire sauce (30 ml)
1 tsp salt (5 ml)
1 tsp pepper (5 ml)
1 c canned mushrooms, including liquid
   (240 ml)
1 Tbsp sugar (15 ml)
2 bay leaves
3 lb cleaned, deveined raw shrimp (2¼ kg)

Melt butter in a large skillet. Add onions, green pepper, celery and garlic and saute until vegetables are soft. Add tomatoes, tomato sauce, Worcestershire sauce, salt, pepper, mushrooms, sugar and bay leaves. Simmer for 45 minutes. Taste, and if the sauce is too tart, add a little more sugar. Add shrimp and simmer for 10 minutes or until shrimp are cooked. Thicken with a little flour and water if a thicker sauce is desired. Serve over rice.

Serves 12.

Calories per serving: approximately 250.

Hank Aaron is a legendary player with the Atlanta Braves.

Dedication to wrestling means maintaining weight by avoiding excess calories, all junk food and foods high in salt. Wrestlers should concentrate on nutritious, low calorie foods and train to keep down total body fat to make their certified weight. The easiest way to control weight is to prevent fluctuation...those victory binges are especially catastrophic.

Studies have shown that wrestlers are able to make more pins and take-downs when they have sufficient calories and fluids to do the job than when they submit to starvation and dehydration to make a lower weight category. On competition days, they should eat breakfast. The rest of the day's meals may be omitted until weigh-in. A small can of any juice and sips of water will give an extra energy boost before mat time.

Like wrestlers, elite competitors in the fields of gym and crew don't tolerate extra fat! Crew members and gymnasts are the lightest and strongest of the lightweights...heavy with muscles, not fat. They depend on nutritionally dense meals to supply required energy.

The problem of weight maintenance lasts through all the years of competition. To make it easier and more tempting, this section contains a variety of low calorie recipes.

Low Calorie Menu Suggestions

Taco Juice**
Calves' Liver with Sweet Basil**
Harvest Vegetables*
Bread Sticks
Fresh Strawberries
Tea or Coffee

Coral Shrimp Dip**
Fresh Vegetable Sticks
Foil Baked Halibut**
Boiled Potatoes with Parsley
Tossed Salad
Cottage Cheese Dressing*
Yogurt Popsicles**
Coffee or Tea

Baked Tarragon Chicken**
Rice
Sukiyaki Salad**
Rhubarb Sauce with Bananas**
Coffee, Tea or Skim Milk

Recipes from wrestling, crew and gymnastics athletes:

Franco Columbo's Mediterranean Omelet*
Franco Columbo's Sardinian Cheesecake*
  Internationally known body builder

Ken Foreman's Bean Salad**
  U.S. Olympic Track and Field Coach

**In this chapter
*See Index

Taco Juice

1 c tomato juice (240 ml)
½ c grated zucchini (120 ml)
Drop of hot sauce
1 tsp lime or lemon juice (5 ml)

Place all ingredients in a blender and blend until smooth. Serve over ice if desired.

Makes 1 generous serving.

Calories per serving: approximately 55.

Coral Shrimp Dip

6½ oz shrimp (200 g)
1 c cottage cheese (240 ml)
3 Tbsp chili sauce (45 ml)
2 Tbsp lemon juice (30 ml)
½ tsp onion juice (3 ml)
¼ tsp Worcestershire sauce (1 ml)

Place all ingredients in a blender, blending until smooth. Chill well. Serve with sliced cucumbers, carrots or celery sticks.

Makes about 2 cups.

Calories per serving: approximately 10.

Cottage Cheese Dressing, with Variations

1 c cottage cheese (240 ml)
⅓ c buttermilk (80 ml)

Mix in blender until smooth.

Variations:

Add 1 Tbsp bleu cheese (15 ml),

or 1 tsp paprika, dry mustard, Worcestershire sauce and thin with tomato juice (5 ml),

or oregano, garlic powder and onion salt to taste,

or anchovies, chopped green onion, parsley and tarragon.

Calories per Tbsp: approximately 20.

Sukiyaki Salad

1 c raw spinach leaves (240 ml)
½ c lettuce (120 ml)
½ c bean sprouts (120 ml)
½ c celery, sliced (120 ml)
¼ c water chestnuts, sliced (60 ml)
½ c fresh mushrooms (120 ml)
½ c green pepper, sliced (120 ml)
½ c cabbage, sliced (120 ml)
1 Tbsp soy sauce (30 ml)
½ c low-cal Italian dressing (120 ml)

Wash spinach and lettuce and tear into bite-size pieces. Combine spinach, lettuce, bean sprouts, celery, water chestnuts, mushrooms, green pepper and cabbage in salad bowl and toss gently. Blend soy sauce and Italian dressing and mix well. Toss. Sliced chicken or fresh shrimp may be added, if desired.

Serves 4-6.

Calories per serving: approximately 100.

Fruit Slaw

3 apples, sliced
2 bananas, sliced
½ c low-cal French dressing (120 ml)
1 c sliced celery (240 ml)
3 c shredded cabbage (720 ml)
½ c fresh orange sections (120 ml)

Combine apples, bananas and French dressing. Add celery, cabbage and orange sections and toss lightly. Refrigerate. This salad will keep for up to 4 hours.

Serves 6.

Calories per serving: approximately 125.

Low-Calorie Pineapple Salad

6 oz lemon-flavored gelatin (180 g)
2 c boiling water (480 ml)
16 oz can grapefruit sections, drained (450 g)
1 c unsweetened crushed pineapple, drained (240 ml)
2 c pineapple-flavored low-fat yogurt (480 ml)
Salad greens

Combine the gelatin with boiling water. Add the drained fruit and mix well. Chill until the mixture is thick. Add yogurt and blend with a rotary beater until yogurt is evenly distributed. Pour into 1½ quart (2 liter) mold and chill until firm. Unmold and garnish with salad greens. For variety, try apricot gelatin mixed with peaches and pears, and peach yogurt.

Serves 8.

Calories per serving: approximately 150.

Lamb Manchu

4 cloves garlic, chopped
⅓ c honey (80 ml)
½ c boiling water (120 ml)
1 c soy sauce (240 ml)
7 lb leg of lamb (3 kg)
½ c white wine (120 ml)

Mix garlic, honey and boiling water, stirring until honey is dissolved. Add soy sauce and pour mixture over lamb. Marinate in refrigerator 12 hours, turning lamb several times. Remove from marinade and place in roasting pan with ½ c (120 ml) of marinade. Cook at 325 °F (165 °C) for 20 minutes (rare) to 30 minutes (well-done) per pound (½ kg). Add wine half-way through the cooking time. Heat remaining marinade in a sauce pan. Slice lamb across the grain and serve with the hot sauce.

Serves about 14.

Calories per serving: approximately 220.

Lamb Kabobs

4 lb lean lamb (1¾ kg)
1½ c cider vinegar (360 ml)
¼ c apricot jam (60 ml)
½ c onion, minced (120 ml)
2 Tbsp curry powder (30 ml)
1 Tbsp salt (15 ml)
3 cloves garlic, minced
¼ c brown sugar (60 ml)
2 bay leaves
½ tsp black pepper (3 ml)
½ tsp cayenne (3 ml)
1 c pineapple chunks (240 ml)
1 c apricot halves (240 ml)
1 c pitted prunes (240 ml)
1 c cantalope pieces (240 ml)

Cut lamb into cubes and place in a large glass bowl. Combine vinegar, jam, onion, curry powder, salt, garlic, brown sugar, bay leaves, pepper and cayenne in a saucepan. Bring to a boil and simmer 5 minutes. Pour over meat; refrigerate and marinate 8-10 hours or overnight. Place meat and fruits on skewers, grill over medium coals, turning to brown all sides. Continually baste with marinade.

Serves 8.

Calories per serving: approximately 370.

Ragout

2 lb lamb shoulder, cubed (1 kg)
1 Tbsp vegetable oil (15 ml)
3 small onions, quartered
1 clove garlic, finely chopped
1 can (16 oz) Italian whole plum tomatoes
1 c beef bouillon (240 ml)
1 tsp salt (5 ml)
Dash of freshly ground pepper
10½ oz frozen green beans (315 g)
Dash of thyme

Brown lamb in hot oil; add onion and garlic and cook 5 minutes. Drain off oil. Add tomatoes, bouillon, salt and pepper. Cover and simmer for 1½ to 2 hours. Just before serving, skim any excess fat, add green beans and thyme and cook until beans are just done.

Serves 6 to 8.

Calories per serving: approximately 240.

Calves Liver and Sweet Basil

1½ lb calves liver, cut into 6 slices (700 g)
½ c flour (120 ml)
6 Tbsp oil (90 ml)
½ c white wine (120 ml)
1 Tbsp sweet basil (15 ml)
2 Tbsp butter (30 ml)

Dip calves liver in flour and saute in oil for 3 minutes on each side. Remove liver to a hot platter, and discard excess oil. Add wine to the pan and stir in all the drippings from the sides and bottom of the pan. Add basil and butter and stir until butter is melted. Pour sauce over liver and serve.

Serves 3-6.

Calories per serving: approximately 225.

Baked Tarragon Chicken

3 lbs chicken pieces (1½ kg)
1 c chicken broth (240 ml)
1 c white wine (240 ml)
½ tsp salt (3 ml)
¼ tsp pepper (1 ml)
1 tsp tarragon (5 ml)
1 clove garlic, sliced

Arrange chicken pieces in a shallow baking pan. Combine broth, wine, salt, pepper, tarragon and sliced garlic in a saucepan. Bring to a boil; boil over medium to high heat until liquid is reduced by one-half (about 5 minutes). Pour hot marinade over chicken pieces. Cover and refrigerate overnight. Bake uncovered in a preheated 400 °F (200 °C) oven for 40 minutes.

Serves 8.

Calories per serving: approximately 215.

Teriyaki Cod

¼ c soy sauce (60 ml)
1 Tbsp brown sugar (15 ml)
2 Tbsp oil (30 ml)
1 tsp flour (5 ml)
1 c dry white wine (240 ml)
½ tsp dry mustard (3 ml)
2 lb white fish (cod, sole, halibut) (1 kg)
6 slices canned pineapple

In saucepan, combine soy sauce, brown sugar, oil, flour, wine and mustard. Bring to boil, reduce heat and simmer for 3 minutes. Cool. Marinate fish for 15 minutes in this liquid. Brush pineapple with marinade and place with the fish on oiled broiling pan. Broil 5 inches (12 cm) from heat for 5 minutes on each side, or until fish flakes easily and is done.

Serves 8.

Calories per serving: approximately 175.

Jack Youngblood's Fillet of Black Cod, Italian Style

4 black cod fillets
8 oz can tomato sauce (225 g)
½ c chopped onion (120 ml)
½ tsp basil (3 ml)
½ tsp oregano (3 ml)
1½ c grated mozzarella cheese (360 ml)

Place fish in greased baking dish. Gently simmer tomato sauce, onion, oregano and basil for 10 minutes in saucepan. Pour over fillets. Bake 20 minutes at 350 °F (175 °C). Sprinkle with cheese and bake an additional 10 minutes.

Serves 4.

Calories per serving: approximately 290.

Jack Youngblood is defensive end for the Los Angeles Rams.

Foil Baked Halibut

16 oz halibut fillets (450 g)
1 tsp salt (5 ml)
¼ tsp pepper (1 ml)
Paprika
4 tsp lemon juice (20 ml)
2 carrots, cut long and slim
1 small green pepper, cut in rings
1 medium onion, sliced
2 tsp butter (10 ml)

Cut fish into 4 servings. Tear off four 1-foot lengths of heavy foil. Center fish portion on each piece of foil. Sprinkle each portion with salt, pepper, paprika and 1 tsp of lemon juice. Divide vegetables between packets, layering on top of fish, and dot with butter. Securely fold. Bake at 450°F (230°C) for 25 minutes.

Serves 4.

Calories per serving: approximately 200.

Stuffed Pocket Sandwiches

1 Tbsp brown sugar (15 ml)
1 Tbsp cornstarch (15 ml)
¾ c water (180 ml)
¼ c teriyaki sauce (60 ml)
¼ c catsup (60 ml)
1 Tbsp lemon juice (15 ml)
1 clove garlic, minced
⅛ tsp ground ginger (1 ml)
2 c cooked chicken, cut in strips (450 g)
1 c bean sprouts (240 ml)
16 oz can mixed Chinese vegetables, drained (450 g)
2 Tbsp sliced green onion (30 ml)
6 pita bread rounds, warm
Shredded lettuce

In medium saucepan, combine brown sugar and cornstarch; stir in water, teriyaki sauce, catsup, lemon juice, garlic, and ginger. Cook and stir until thickened and bubbly. Stir in chicken, bean sprouts, drained vegetables, and onion; heat through. Halve pita rounds; spoon in meat mixture and top with lettuce.

Serves 6.

Calories per serving: approximately 230.

Harvest Vegetables

1 bunch of broccoli
1 small head of cauliflower
1 Tbsp fresh lemon juice (15 ml)
2 c sliced mushrooms (480 ml)
1 Tbsp oil (15 ml)
1 green pepper, sliced lengthwise
2 c celery, sliced diagonally (480 ml)
1 clove minced garlic
1 tsp onion salt (5 ml)
1 tsp freshly ground pepper (5 ml)
2 Tbsp soy sauce (30 ml)
½ c grated low-fat Cheddar cheese (120 ml)

Trim stems and leaves from broccoli and cauliflower; divide into flowerettes. Pour lemon juice over mushrooms and set aside. Cook broccoli and cauliflower for 3-5 minutes, or until just tender. Measure oil into large skillet and heat to medium high. Add all vegetables and seasonings except soy sauce and stir fry for 5 minutes, or until vegetables are cooked, but still crisp. Add soy sauce and cheese.

Serves 8.

Calories per serving: approximately 60.

Rhubarb Sauce with Bananas

3 c rhubarb, cut in chunks (720 ml)
¼ c sugar (60 ml)
¼ c water (60 ml)
Artificial sweetener to taste
4 bananas, sliced

Combine rhubarb, sugar and water; bring to boil and cook for 5 minutes. Add artificial sweetener if desired. Serve hot or cold over bananas.

Serves 6.

Calories per serving: approximately 100.

Yogurt Popsicles

8 oz plain yogurt (240 g)
6 oz concentrated fruit juice (180 g)
½ tsp vanilla

Mix ingredients well. Pour mixture into 3 oz paper cups with plastic spoon inserted. Freeze. Can be doubled or tripled.

Serves 6.

Calories per serving: approximately 70.

Whipped Powdered Dry Milk

When a recipe calls for a whipped cream topping and you'd like to eliminate a few calories, try this:

½ c powdered dry milk (120 ml)
¼ c ice water (60 ml)
2 Tbsp lemon juice (30 ml)
1 Tbsp sugar (15 ml)

Combine instant dry milk and ice water in a chilled bowl and whip at high speed for about 4 minutes until soft peaks are formed. Add lemon juice and then sugar, and then continue whipping until stiff. Refrigerate until time to use.

Yield: 2½ cups (600 ml).

Calories per Tbsp: approximately 10.

Ken Foreman's Bean Salad

2 c French green beans (480 ml)
2 c red kidney beans (480 ml)
6½ oz white tuna (195 gm)
1 c artichoke hearts (240 ml)
1 c water chestnuts, sliced (240 ml)
2 Tbsp red onion (30 ml)
1 small green onion, chopped
½ c green pepper, chopped (120 ml)
½ c sugar (120 ml)
⅔ c vinegar (160 ml)
⅓ c salad oil (80 ml)
¼ tsp salt (1 ml)

Drain beans and add to tuna, artichoke hearts, water chestnuts, onions and green pepper. Mix sugar, vinegar, oil and salt and bring to a boil. Pour over bean mixture. Chill for several hours. To decrease calories, use low calorie Italian dressing for marinade instead of the sugar, vinegar & oil.

Serves 8-10.

Calories per serving: 170.

Ken Foreman is the 1980 U.S. Olympic Track and Field Coach for women.

Mushroom and Sprout Salad

1 lb fresh mushrooms (450 g)
¼ c fresh lemon juice (60 ml)
¼ c olive oil (60 ml)
1 tsp salt (5 ml)
½ tsp pepper (3 ml)
2 tsp sugar (10 ml)
1 tsp dill weed (5 ml)
¼ c chopped parsley (60 ml)
¼ c minced green onions (60 ml)
2 c alfalfa sprouts (480 ml)

Slice mushrooms and add lemon juice, oil, salt, pepper, sugar and dill weed. Let marinate for 1 hour or more. Just before serving, add parsley, onion and alfalfa sprouts. Toss together gently. Use as a salad or first course.

Serves 6.

Calories per serving: approximately 70.

I. To calculate your maintenance level:
    A. Look up the "normal" or "ideal" weight for your height and build. Remember, an athlete does not always fit the chart specifications because of muscle development.
    B. Multiply this "ideal" weight by:
        1) 15—if adult, sedentary
        2) 20—if adult, active
        3) 30—if adolescent, active
    C. Add calories if expended in extra activity. Figure minutes of activity and cost per minute.
    D. This gives an approximate level of energy intake. For example: Female, 5'4", slight frame:

1) Ideal weight	108 lbs
2) Adult, active	x 20
	2,160
3) Running (12 min. at 5 mph)	+ 120
4) Desired calorie level is:	2,280

II. To lose weight:
    A. To lose ¾ lb/week (3-4 lb per month), decrease food intake 500 cal per day below approximate needs.
    B. To lose 2 lb/week (6-8 lb/month), decrease food intake 1,000 cal per day below approximate needs.
    C. It is advisable to lose only 1-2 lb/week as too rapid a weight loss causes irritability, decreased reaction time, decreased concentration ability and insomnia.

III. To gain weight:
    A. To gain 1 lb/week, increase food intake 500 cal per day above needs.
    B. To gain 2 lb/week, increase food intake 1,000 cal per day above needs.
    C. Too rapid a gain will usually result in a deposition of fat instead of muscle tissue. Muscle development will occur if favored by gradual gain in weight and a regular exercise program.

Calorie/Exercise Guide *

Desirable weights for MEN of ages 25 and over Weights in pounds according to frame (in indoor clothing)			
Height (Shoes on 1″ heels)	Small Frame	Medium Frame	Large Frame
5′2″	112-120	118-129	126-141
5′3″	115-123	121-133	129-144
5′4″	118-126	124-136	132-148
5′5″	121-129	127-139	135-152
5′6″	124-133	130-143	138-156
5′7″	128-137	134-147	142-161
5′8″	132-141	138-152	147-166
5′9″	136-145	142-156	151-170
5′10″	140-150	146-160	155-174
5′11″	144-154	150-165	159-179
6′0″	148-158	154-170	164-184
6′1″	152-162	158-175	168-189
6′2″	156-167	162-180	173-194
6′3″	160-171	167-185	178-199
6′4″	164-175	172-190	182-204

Desired weights for WOMEN of ages 25 and over For girls between 18 and 25, subtract 1 pound for each year under 25			
Height (Shoes on 2″ heels)	Small Frame	Medium Frame	Large Frame
4′10″	92-98	96-107	104-119
4′11″	94-101	98-110	106-122
5′0″	96-104	101-113	109-125
5′1″	99-107	104-116	112-128
5′2″	102-110	107-119	115-131
5′3″	105-113	110-122	118-134
5′4″	108-116	113-126	121-138
5′5″	111-119	116-130	125-142
5′6″	114-123	120-135	129-146
5′7″	118-127	124-139	133-150
5′8″	122-131	128-143	137-154
5′9″	126-135	132-147	141-158
5′10″	130-140	136-151	145-163
5′11″	134-144	140-155	149-168
6′0″	138-148	144-159	153-173

*Courtesy of Metropolitan Life Insurance Company

Caloric Expenditure During Various Activities

Activity	Calories/Min (Approximate)
Sleeping	1.2
Sitting	1.3
Standing	1.5
Standing, light activity	2.6
Driving a car	2.8
Driving a motorcycle	3.4
Gardening	5.6
Chopping wood	7.5
Walking Upstairs	10.0-18.0
Pool or billiards	1.8
Canoeing 2.5-4.0 MPH	3.0-7.0
Volleyball, Recreational—Comp	3.5-8.0
Golf, Foursome-Twosome	3.7-5.0
Horseshoes	3.8
Baseball	4.7
Ping Pong, Table Tennis	4.9-7.0
Calisthenics	5.0
Rowing, Pleasure—Vigorous	5.0-15.0
Cycling, 5-15 MPH (10 speed)	5.0-12.0
Skating, Recreation—Vigorous	5.0-15.0
Archery	5.2
Badminton, Recreation—Comp	5.2-10.0
Basketball, Half, Full Court	6.0-9.0
Bowling (while active)	7.0
Tennis, Recreational—Comp	7.0-11.0
Water Skiing	8.0
Soccer	9.0
Snowshoeing 2.5 MPH	9.0
Handball and Squash	10.0
Mountain Climbing	10.0
Skipping Rope	10.0-15.0
Judo and Karate	13.0
Football (while active)	13.3
Wrestling	14.4

Skiing:
Moderate to Steep	8.0-12.0
Downhill Racing	16.5
Cross-Country 3-8 MPH	9.0-17.0

Swimming:
Pleasure	6.0
Vigorous, 25-50 yds/min	6.0-12.5

Dancing:
Modern, Moderate—Vigorous	4.2-5.7
Square	7.1

Walking:
Road-Field 3.5 MPH	5.6-7.0
Uphill 5-10-15% 3.5 MPH	8.0-11.0-15.0
Hiking, 40 lb. pack 3.0 MPH	6.8

Running:
12 min mile 5 MPH	10.0
8 min mile 7.5 MPH	15.0
6 min mile 10 MPH	20.0
5 min mile 12 MPH	25.0

Sources: Consolazio, Johnson & Pecora, 1963; Human Performance Laboratory (Sharkey) University of Montana, 1964-1978; Passmore & Durnin, 1955; Roth, 1968.

Sources of Reliable Information

American College of Sports Medicine
1440 Monroe St.
Madison, Wisconsin   53706

American Dental Association
222 E. Superior Street
Chicago, Illinois   60611

American Dietetic Assocation
430 N. Michigan Avenue
Chicago, Illinois   60611

American Institute of Baking
400 E. Ontario Street
Chicago, Illinois   60611

American Medical Association
535 N. Dearborn Street
Chicago, Illinois   60610

Borden Co.
350 Madison Avenue
New York, New York   10017

Cereal Institute
135 S. LaSalle Street
Chicago, Illinois   60603

National Academy of Sciences
National Research Council
2101 Constitution Avenue
Washington, D.C.   20418

National Dairy Council
111 N. Canal Street
Chicago, Illinois   60606

National Meat and Livestock Board
36 Wabash Avenue
Chicago, Illinois   60603

The Nutrition Foundation, Inc.
489 Fifth Avenue
New York, New York   10016

Society for Nutrition Education
2140 Shattuck Avenue
Suite 1110
Berkeley, California   94704

Superintendent of Documents
U.S. Government Printing Office
Washington, D.C.   20250

U.S. Department of Agriculture
Washington, D.C.   20250

Selected Bibliography

American Association for Health, Physical Education, and Recreation. **Nutrition for Athletes. A Handbook for Coaches.** Washington, D.C.: 1971.

Astrand, P.. "Nutrition and Physical Performance." In: **World Review of Nutrition and Dietetics**, Vol. I6. Edited by M. Rechcigl. Washington: S. Karger, 1973.

Astrand, P. and Rodahl, K.. **Textbook of Work Physiology.** New York: McGraw-Hill Book Co., 1970.

Bogert, L. Jean; Briggs, G.M. and Calloway, D.H.. **Nutrition and Physical Fitness.** 9th ed. Philadelphia: W.B. Saunders Co., 1973.

Church, C.F., and Church, H.N.. **Food Values of Portions Commonly Used.** Philadelphia: J.B. Lippincott Co., 1975.

Consolazio, C.F.. "Nutrition and The Athletic Performance." In: **Progress In Human Nutrition**, Vol. I. Edited by S. Margen. Westport, Conn.: AVI Publishing Co., 1971.

Lewis, S., and Gutin, B.. "Nutrition and Endurance." In: **American Journal of Clinical Nutrition,** 26. 1973.

Mathews, D.K. and Fox, E.L.. **Physiologic Basis of Physical Education and Athletes.** Philadelphia, PA: W.B. Saunders, 1971.

Mayer, J. and Bullen, B.. "Nutrition and The Athletic Performance." In: **Physiological Reviews.** 40. 1960.

Index

Marilyn Shope Peterson, M.S., R.D., Nutritionist for the Sports Medicine Clinic, Seattle, Washington, has acted as nutritional consultant to the U.S. Olympic team. She met her husband on the football field; they are now feeding four young athletes of their own.

Charlene S. Martinsen, Ph.D., R.D., Associate Professor of Nutritional Sciences at the University of Washington in Seattle, is the author of many cookbooks, including the bestseller, **Gourmet Grains**. She is the mother of a young athlete who very much likes to run.

Having spent more than thirty years coaching, I can attest to the fact that eating the proper things at the right time is of fundamental importance to successful performance. **The Athlete's Cookbook** *is a practical nutritional guide...Perhaps its greatest value is its simplicity and usefulness in meal planning on a daily basis.*

Ken Foreman, Head Coach
U.S. Olympic Team, Woman's Athletics
From the Introduction

This cookbook is for active people of all ages. It is an informative nutritional guide well as a collection of recipe that range from quick snacks and delicious desserts to hea main dishes.

Marilyn Peterson, nutritioni for the Sports Medicine Clinic in Seattle, has acted as nutritional consultant to the U.S. Olympic Team. Charlene Martinsen teaches nutritional science at the University of Washington and is the author of the bestselling cookbook, **Gourmet Grains**.

ISBN 0-918484-05-7 $8.95